THE POSTURE OF
A GODLY LEADER

Coming soon in the *Starting Right in Church Revitalization Series*:

The Posture of a Godly Leader, Mark Hallock

Foundational Priorities of a Biblical Church, Mark Hallock

Intentional Practices for Effective Ministry, Mark Hallock

Persevering in Pastoral Faithfulness, Mark Hallock

THE
POSTURE
OF A GODLY LEADER

MARK HALLOCK
FOREWORD BY DUFFY ROBBINS

ACOMA PRESS

STARTING RIGHT IN CHURCH REVITALIZATION

CONTENTS

ACKNOWLEDGEMENTS

I want to thank a few important individuals who played a vital role in the shaping and writing of this book.

I want to thank my wonderful wife, Jenna, and my children Zoe and Eli. Thank you for your constant encouragement in my life and ministry. I love you.

Thank you to Kim Grady who helped me immensely in making edits for this book. You are not only a gifted writer but a dear friend.

Thank you to Ruth Piotrowski who sacrificed many hours to make this book what it is. I am so grateful. You are a true servant of the Lord.

Thank you to Evan Skelton, a great designer, but an even better pastor.

Thank you to Duffy Robbins, a great friend and mentor for many years. Your fingerprints are all over these pages. Thank you for investing in me and so many other pastors.

I praise God for the gift it is to serve the Lord alongside each of you. *Soli Deo Gloria.*

Mark Hallock

FORWARD

You've likely never heard of Tim Noble or Sue Webster. Two artists, both based in London, they are among a growing tribe of artists who work in a medium sometimes called Found Art. It's a remarkable field of artistic endeavor in which artists create works - sometimes stunning, sometimes humorous, sometimes even a little silly - out of little more than found objects. It might be sea shells, or scrap iron, or random buttons, or kidnapped hotel towels, or plastic spoons, or even cigarette butts. Noble and Webster basically work with trash - from what I can tell, all kinds of trash. I wonder how many Brits have gone to a Noble and Webster exhibit and thought, "Holy cow, that looks like the bedroom slipper I threw out last year because the dog chewed it up!" Their most stunning pieces feature massive mounds of garbage piled in just such a way that, when the pile is exposed to light, what we see in the shadow is a surprising image of intricacy and detail.

One of the reasons I'm so intrigued by Found Art is because, consciously or not, it tells the story of redemption. I, for one, have seen the wonder of what God can do when I'm willing to give him my junk, and willingly expose it to His light. It is the gracious surprise of a God who brings life to the dying, who takes what was essentially trash and redeems it into a new creation.

Mark Hallock is a found artist. He and his team at Calvary have a vision for what God can do with dying churches that are exposed to the vivid light of Christ's love and grace. The images that have resulted from this ministry, images of vibrant, growing, revitalized churches, are both stunning and wonderful, and they point to the artistry of God and the fruit of imaginative, faithful leadership.

Both in Found Art and in revitalizing churches, we are reminded of some fundamental truths that those of us in pastoral ministry would do well to remember. We're reminded of these truths:

#1. New isn't always better than old, but reviving is always better than dying.

In an age when most of our instincts are to trash the old church on the corner, it's easy to fall into the trap of thinking that what we need is something "new" - new spaces, new church names, a new message, new cool people singing new cool songs bathed in cool new lighting. But, revitalized churches remind us that ours is a God of renewal and resurrection, and that a True Gospel always brings more light than a new strategy. Our best play in pastoral ministry is not to rearrange the garbage; it's to shine on it the light of God's Word and Spirit.

#2. There's always the possibility of new life.

God can bring amazing surprises out of even the ugliest circumstances. That's why it's always too soon to give up on the Church. That means we need leaders who can see a Masterpiece in the midst of the mess, a jewel in the pile of junk, a refuge of grace in the often unpleasant refuse of everyday church life. There has to be a visionary artist who is willing to pain-stakingly and lovingly bring beauty and color and vibrancy to something that everybody else declared done and over and ready for the dumpster. Found Artists and Revitalizing pastors see hope and possibility in unlikely places. And we desperately need more of these leaders and churches who believe God is a Redeemer.

#3. Brokenness can be a doorway to beauty.

The key, of course, is that Found Art has to get found. It cannot assemble itself. In other words, step one is helplessness, a core humility, a recognition that everything is rewired, plugged in, turned on, but somehow we're not getting the sound or the Light that brings authentic change and new life. We wonder why people are more likely to Google the "Christmas wreath made out of cigarette butts" than to show up on Sunday morning because they've heard about "...this amazing thing the people of God have created". And, in truth it's because we've neglected to plug in to the true power Source. So, we begin with the simple, clear understanding that what we're doing, or what we've become, is not working. It's only in that honest confession of need that the door opens for beauty, healing and revival to enter the building.

FOUND ARTISTS AND REVITALIZING PASTORS

In this book, Mark Hallock answers, then, the obvious question: **What sort of artists/pastors/leaders do we need to bring worship, community and service to dying churches?** And in very practical terms he inventories both the traits and the skills needed for this sort of ministry. This is not just a book you read through; it's a book you pray through. You will find instruction in these chapters, good instruction by a guy whose writing is shaped by real-world pastoral experience. But, along with the instruction will come inspiration and exhortation, words of encouragement from a fellow pastor who is pressing on for the prize and seeking to live out the very words of his own text.

What gave me tremendous hope and promise as I read through this book is the reminder that godly pastors - all of us - are ourselves works of found art. We are, in the hands of the Potter, being molded and shaped even as we do our work of reviving and rebuilding. Which is why I think this book is so helpful. It reminds us of what Eugene Peterson calls "the shape of pastoral integrity": what it means to lead with humility, love, patience, faith, passion and joy. And to do it with the sort of gracious artistry that understands the colors and textures of servanthood, the lights and darks of pastoral work, and that essential eye for being able to see grace in the midst of the garbage.

My prayer, as you read this book, is that you would hear in the words of my friend, Mark Hallock, a challenge not to pursue the new strategy, but pursue revival; a reminder not to forget that God can bring life even in your struggling, limping, aging congregation, of whom it's so easy to declare "expired", and an invitation to recognize that if we expose our brokenness to God's Light, He can bring gracious surprises of wonder and redemption to our ministries. And that it all starts with the Spirit working in Godly pastors and leaders who understand that we ourselves are His workmanship.

> "For we are his workmanship, created in Christ Jesus for good works, which God prepared beforehand, that we should walk in them." Ephesians 2: 9-10

Duffy Robbins
Grove City College, Grove City, PA

INTRODUCTION

This is a book about leadership.

Now as soon as you read that, if you are like me, you're thinking, "Seriously? Another book on leadership? I already have a shelf full of leadership books thank you very much."

I get it. I'm with you. The last thing you need is to read yet another book on leadership. Truth is, there are so many great leadership books out there, why in the world would I even take the time to write this little volume?

Here's why. I have a specific burden.

The longer I am in ministry, the clearer it becomes just how important strong leadership in the church is, and this is particularly true when it comes to pastoral leadership in struggling, declining congregations. And there lies the burden of this book: How to best lead dying churches back to life.

What kind of leadership is needed to guide a dying church back to life? Or, put another way, what are those leadership qualities that make a church revitalizer most effective?

Perhaps many different qualities jump to your mind. You might think of such things as personal charisma or cultural savvy or speaking ability or programming creativity or strategic planning. These are the types of things that often pop up in conversations surrounding this topic. Don't get me wrong, each of these has its place. And there is no question that qualities like these can be very helpful and at times are quite necessary in church revitalization. But in this book, I want to go in a different direction. I want to dive a little bit deeper. I want to intentionally go beneath the surface of leadership methodology and strategy, as important as these are, and look at the leader's heart. Specifically, the heart of those leading hurting, struggling, weary, tired, dying churches.

What I am most concerned with in these pages is not "what" to do as a pastor leading a declining church but rather "how" a pastor is to rightly lead a declining church. I'm not concerned so much with the most effective "practices" (though I will include many of those) but rather the "posture" a God-honoring church revitalizer must lead with and from.

I'm convinced that leading a dying church back to health and vibrancy, by the power of the Holy Spirit, is unlike any other calling in ministry. It involves some of the biggest challenges and yet some of the greatest joys a pastor could ever experience in service to Christ and His people. For this reason, I believe there are some unique leadership qualities needed for a revitalization pastor to truly succeed. Specifically, there are six that I want to focus on in this book. When I am asked, "What does it take for a pastor to effectively lead a dying church back to life?", what automatically jumps to my mind are these six characteristics:

- ○ Humility
- ○ Patience
- ○ Love
- ○ Faith
- ○ Passion
- ○ Joy

Listen, as a church revitalizer, you can be gifted in all kinds of leadership areas, but without these six characteristics, and I say this in love, you will struggle to be:

- **The kind of pastor and leader that people actually want to follow,** not simply have to follow.

- **The kind of pastor and leader that leads real change** by the power of the Spirit in the lives of individuals, churches, and entire communities.

- **The kind of pastor and leader that brings glory to God** as one who faithfully shepherds the sheep Jesus died for and paid for with His own blood.

I hope you want to be this kind of pastor and leader because this is the kind of pastor and leader dying churches all across North America and around the world desperately need! More than that, this is the kind of pastor and leader God has called you and empowered you to be for His glory.

TWO CLARIFIERS

There are two things I want to briefly mention, which I think are helpful for you to know. First of all, the danger of writing any book, let alone a book like this one, is that the author runs the temptation and risk of coming off like an expert on the topic. I want to make it perfectly clear from the very beginning that I am not an expert in the things I write about in this book. I am in process just like you are. While the Lord has graciously taught me (and continues to teach me) many things about leadership over my years serving in the local church, I have much to learn! I mean that. My hope in writing this little book is to simply share some of what God has taught me, and continues to teach me, from His Word, as one called to pastor and lead His people.

Secondly, while the primary audience of this book are those called to help lead and revitalize declining and dying churches, I do believe much of the content here can be helpful to those serving in other areas of ministry and leadership too. In many ways, this book applies to anyone stepping into a leadership position with an existing ministry or organization. In particular, an existing ministry or organization that is plateaued or declining. So, whether you are a youth pastor called to lead a student ministry that is struggling, a worship leader trying to lead a healthy transition within a congregation's music ministry, or a volunteer desiring to take your ministry team to the next level, I believe this book can be of help to you on some level in your leadership.

HOW TO GET THE MOST OUT OF THIS BOOK

Before we get started, let me offer three suggestions to help you get the most out of this book:

#1. Take your time. At the end of each chapter, I have provided a set of questions and exercises for personal reflection and discussion. To get the most out of this book, you will want to set aside intentional, unrushed time to pray through and meditate on these. This time of thoughtful and prayerful reflection will be important as you seek to digest and then integrate the material of each chapter into your life and leadership.

#2. Buy a journal…and use it! I highly recommend picking up a journal of some sort to record your thoughts, prayers, and meditations as you work through this book. It will be helpful to have all of your thoughts in one place as you journal and interact with the questions and exercises. Your journal will also be useful as you interact with others about what you are reading and learning.

#3. Think about inviting someone to join you. While you might choose to work through this book on your own, you may also want to consider asking someone to read it with you. There can be great value in asking your spouse, a pastor, a mentor, a friend, or a fellow church revitalizer to join you in your study. So often God uses other people to help us grow. This is particularly true in our growth as leaders. Other people in your life can bring helpful insight and perspective you could never get on your own.

THE STARTING RIGHT IN CHURCH REVITALIZATION BOOK SERIES

The Posture of a Godly Leader is the first in a four-book series focusing on the ministry of church revitalization. The series, *Starting Right in Church Revitalization,* focuses on key areas of pastoral ministry crucial in turning around a declining church. The goal of this series is to help educate, equip, and encourage pastors and leaders called specifically to serve these congregations. Each book is aimed at helping individuals start well in their ministry, building a strong foundation that will help bring long term health, growth, and multiplication to dying churches in North America and to the ends of the earth.

As you now dive into *The Posture of a Godly Leader*, my prayer is that the Lord will both encourage you and challenge you to be the pastor and leader He has made you to be. That He will use this little book to sharpen you and help you mature and grow in leading with a Christ-like heart. Posture is everything when it comes to leading in a biblical, God-honoring manner. May your leadership posture be increasingly conformed to the very posture of Christ Himself.

For the good of His Church and the fame of His name.
Mark Hallock

CHAPTER 1

HUMILITY

THE FOUNDATION OF GODLY LEADERSHIP

"God opposes the proud but gives grace to the humble."
- James 4:6b

"Everyone who exalts himself will be humbled, and he who humbles himself will be exalted."
- Luke 14:11

I was having lunch with an older pastor friend of mine a while back, and we began talking about what makes a great pastor. Specifically, we discussed those things that tend to mark pastors who are faithful—for the long haul—to both the Lord and the flock under their care.

This particular friend devotedly shepherded the same congregation for nearly 40 years. 40 years! So, you can imagine, if there is one guy from whom I am always eager to learn, it is him. He doesn't just theorize about what it means to be a great pastor. He *is* a great pastor. And he lived it faithfully week in and week out over the course of decades.

As we visited about the importance of faithfully preaching the Word, loving people well, and leading a congregation with compelling vision and deep conviction, he shared what he believed was unquestionably one of the most important characteristics of a great pastor: humility. He said, "Without humility before God and other people, it simply doesn't matter how gifted you are in every other area of pastoral ministry. You will fail." He continued, "I really believe that genuine, Christlike humility is what earns trust and wins the hearts of people more than anything else as a leader in the church. In a world where we tend to elevate leaders who are powerful and prideful, Christ calls pastors to lead with humility."

My pastor friend is right. While we don't talk about it nearly enough, one of the most important attributes in the heart of a godly pastor and leader is humility. If we are not individuals who are humble before the Lord and humble before people, we have no business pastoring and shepherding a struggling and hurting local church. That is the bottom line.

God says a lot about humility in His Word. In fact, what we see throughout Scripture is that God will oppose the proud, but He loves to give grace to the humble. He loves to show mercy to those who know they are simply servants of the Lord, nothing more and nothing less. Again, James puts it this way in chapter 4, verse 6, "God opposes the proud but gives grace to the humble." Humility is what the Lord is looking for in His leaders.

The same is true for churches—in particular, dying and declining churches. Churches that are prideful and refuse to humble themselves before the Lord are not in a good spot. The Lord will oppose these kinds of churches. I don't know about you, but the last thing I want to be is opposed by God as an individual or church because of our pride! What a scary thought this is! And it should be. The truth is, the Lord exalts and uniquely blesses leaders and churches that humble themselves before Him. Humility is a big deal to God. It must be a big deal to us too.

JESUS ON HUMILITY

In Mark 9:33–35, we see an example of how Jesus viewed the importance of humility. One day, our Lord was traveling through Galilee on the way to Capernaum with His disciples, His closest friends. Imagine the scene. Just out of earshot of Jesus—or so they thought—the disciples challenged each other about who was going to be first in the Kingdom of God and with whom Jesus was going to be the most impressed.

> And they came to Capernaum, and when he was in the house, he asked them, "What were you discussing on the way?" But they kept silent, for on the way they had argued with one another about who was the greatest. And he sat down and called the twelve. And he said them, "If anyone would be first, he must be last of all and servant of all."

We see this discussion arise again in Luke 22:24-27, only this time during the Passover feast. Jesus had broken the bread with them and had foretold Judas' betrayal. The discussion quickly jumped from who was the traitor to who would be the greatest.

> A dispute also arose among them, as to which of them was to be regarded as the greatest. And he said to them, "The kings of the Gentiles exercise lordship over them, and those in authority over them are called benefactors. But not so with you. Rather, let the greatest among you become as the youngest, and the leader as

one who serves. For who is the greater, one who reclines at table or one who serves? Is it not the one who reclines at table? But I am among you as the one who serves.

Jesus is not impressed with big egos, especially in His leaders. He is not impressed by overconfidence in oneself. He is not impressed with any desires people might have to put themselves above others. No, Jesus is pleased with pastors and leaders who intentionally put themselves last for the sake of serving everyone else.

Jesus demonstrated this kind of humble, servant leadership when He washed His disciples' feet the night before He would be put to death. He wanted to show them how to humbly serve others. This is what the best leaders do. They put those whom they lead above themselves. They wash their feet. Jesus took off His outer garment, wrapped a towel around His waist like a servant, knelt on the floor and, with some protest from Peter, washed the dirty, grimy feet of His disciples. In John 13:12-16, Jesus speaks to His disciples,

> Do you understand what I have done to you? You call me Teacher and Lord, and you are right, for so I am. If I then, your Lord and Teacher, have washed your feet, you also ought to wash one another's feet. For I have given you an example, that you also should do just as I have done to you. Truly, truly, I say to you, a servant is not greater than his master, nor is a messenger greater than the one who sent him.

Jesus displays what servant leadership looks like through washing His disciples' feet. Ultimately, we see the humble, servant heart of Jesus in His leaving the comforts of heaven and becoming a man. In the incarnation, Jesus, the God-Man, humbled Himself to serve and to save sinners through His life and atoning death on the cross.

Exhorting believers to follow Christ's example of humility, the Apostle Paul writes in Philippians 2:1-8,

> So if there is any encouragement in Christ, any comfort from love, any participation in the Spirit, any affection and sympathy, complete my joy by being of the same mind, having the same love, being in full accord and of one mind. Do nothing from selfish ambition or conceit, but in humility count others more significant than yourselves. Let each of you look not only to his own interests, but also to the interests of others. Have this mind among yourselves, which is yours in Christ Jesus, who, though he was in the form of God, did not count equality with God a thing to be grasped, but emptied himself, by taking the form of a servant, being born in the likeness of men. And being found in human form, he humbled himself by becoming obedient to the point of death, even death on a cross.

We see in the life and example of Jesus what God wants in His people—specifically, in His pastors and leaders. Humility. God is drawn to humility. As revitalization pastors, we must approach our calling with this kind of deep, Spirit-empowered humility. The good news, of course, is that Christ not only serves as our primary example of what humility looks like, He also serves as our source of power to live it out in our own lives and leadership. May we seek His face daily, that He might give us a humble heart like His.

HUMILITY IN CHURCH REVITALIZATION

When we think about serving the Lord and His people—in particular, seeking to help lead a declining church back to health and vibrancy—what exactly should humility look like? Practically speaking, what does humble, pastoral leadership look like in this context? Let me propose several ways to practice humble leadership as a revitalizer. As you read, reflect on your own leadership and your own heart posture. How are you doing in these areas? Where do you need the Lord to grow you?

Don't wear a title as a way to show you're in charge.

Being a pastor and leader in the church is not about power. It is not about being a force to be reckoned with—throwing out our title, bragging about what we do or what we have done, or seeking to display whatever perceived authority we think we might have. These are all marks of an immature, prideful pastor and leader. It is the opposite of what Christ calls us to. We are undershepherds of the Good Shepherd. We are servants of the Chief Servant, charged to place ourselves under—not over—the flock. This is the kind of humble leadership that Jesus calls us to live out and exemplify by the Spirit's power. Peter puts it this way in 1 Peter 5:1-4:

> So I exhort the elders among you, as a fellow elder and a witness of the sufferings of Christ, as well as a partaker in the glory that is going to be revealed: shepherd the flock of God that is among you, exercising oversight, not under compulsion, but willingly, as God would have you; not for shameful gain, but eagerly; not domineering over those in your charge, but being examples to the flock. And when the chief Shepherd appears, you will receive the unfading crown of glory.

Bottom line: Never wear a title as a way to show you're in charge.

Don't do everything.

We can't do everything as pastors. We were never intended to. So, pastor friend, don't even try! We are part of a beautifully diverse body of believers, made up of all kinds and types of people with different gifts, talents, and passions. What a glorious thing this is! In Romans 12:3-8, Paul reminds us of the beauty of this diversity:

> For by the grace given to me I say to everyone among you not to think of himself more highly than he ought to think, but to think with sober judgment, each according to the measure of faith that God has assigned. For as in one body we have many members, and the members do not all have the same function, so we, though many, are one body in Christ, and individually members one of another. Having gifts that differ according to the grace given to us, let us use them: if prophecy, in proportion to our faith; if service, in our serving; the one who teaches, in his teaching; the one who exhorts, in his exhortation; the one who contributes, in generosity; the one who leads, with zeal; the one who does acts of mercy, with cheerfulness.

As pastors in a declining church, we can't do it all alone. Even better, God designed it this way. We need to be regularly reminded of this fact, humbly and eagerly at work to get others involved in using their gifts. We must seek to intentionally equip and encourage the saints for the work of ministry as the Word instructs us to do (Ephesians 4:12-16).

Leading by example, we should strive to make Jesus—not ourselves—the hero in our churches. Sadly, I have witnessed pastors who, out of deep insecurity and the need to be needed, fail to raise up and unleash other leaders in their churches. They feel threatened by other leaders. They want to maintain absolute control over what those in the congregation do and don't do. They refuse to share the spotlight with anyone else, including Jesus Himself. This is troubling on a number of levels and for a number of reasons. Sadly, over time, these types of pastors wear people out, and they run people off. They quench the work of the Spirit in their congregations. All of this stems from a lack of humility before God and others—a humility that says, "I can't do it all, nor was I ever meant to."

An egotistical, controlling leader who fails to raise up others and share ministry with the people of God is the last thing a dying church needs. The last thing. Instead, with humble hearts, we as pastors must develop and deploy others to lead alongside us. This involves intentional, joyful delegation. When we struggle with various areas of ministry (and we will!), let us ask the Lord to help us say to others, *I'm not good at this. Would you be willing to help me?*" Over time, we will realize that there are plenty of other people who have skill sets and gifts that we lack. That is okay! More than okay, it is wonderful! It is the Lord's design. As pastors, we are one part of the body, called to encourage other parts of the body to use their gifts for the glory of God and for the good of others.

Give others a platform to lead and influence.

When we enter a church revitalization context, we are most likely going to meet very tired folks, most of whom are discouraged for one reason or another. What an opportunity this is for us to love them, encourage them, and speak words of hope to them! If we want to see individuals like these gain renewed life and passion for the Lord and for ministry, we must express how much we value them. And we must do this a lot. We must brag on others, from little kids to adults, both publicly and privately. We must build others up through our words and actions, working to draw out their gifts and ministry dreams that perhaps have been stunted for a long time.

The platform of influence that we maintain as pastors and leaders is not ours. It belongs to Jesus. This means we must appropriately steward whatever platform He has given us, for His purposes and for His ultimate glory. Use your platform for the sake of Christ and others. Give others a voice. Give others influence. Give others the chance to use their gifts and abilities to show Jesus off themselves.

This is what humble leaders do.

Be quick to give credit to others and just as quick to take the blame.

The best leaders in the church are those who are quick to give credit to others, even if they themselves are the ones who deserve it. They are just as quick to take the blame, even if they're not the ones at fault.

As pastors, this humble commitment falls on us. If we constantly have a defensive posture or are regularly trying to pass the blame off on someone else, our congregations will not follow us with love and trust. No one wants to follow that kind of leader. Followers, however, are drawn to humble leaders who have the kind of integrity that prompts them to sacrifice themselves for the good of others. For the good of the church. For the good of the Gospel. These are the kinds of leaders we must strive to be in church revitalization. We must keep our eyes fixed on Jesus. He who knew no sin went to the cross, taking our sins and our blame upon Himself, thus demonstrating the ultimate sacrificial leadership for the sake of others. Therefore, we must be prepared to humbly and joyfully follow Jesus' example—to give credit to others and to take the blame even when we don't deserve it.

The key to actually living this out is growing in both understanding and application of the Gospel to our own lives. Growing to be more and more confident that our identity is in

Christ and His approval of us, not in the approval of others. Maturing in our understanding of what it means to be secure in who we are as His children, if we are in Him. As these truths become more deeply rooted in our hearts and minds, we will grow in our eagerness to give credit and to take blame in the way a truly humble leader should.

Do the things no one else wants to do... and do them joyfully, with a servant's heart.

As a church revitalizer, you are called to be a generalist, at least on some level. This means you need to be ready and prepared to do the things that no one else wants to do—and do them joyfully. And there are some crazy things that need to be done.

Cleaning toilets and taking the trash out is no fun for anybody in the church, but someone has to do it. Oftentimes, we as pastors need to take the lead in making sure whatever needs to get done, gets done. This is true even when the things that most need to get done are our least favorite things to do in the world.

In the very beginning stages of your time serving as a new pastor, everybody is watching you. They are listening to you. They are watching what you do and what you don't do. They are listening to what you say and what you don't say. Whether you like it or not, they're going to make a judgment within the first few months as to what kind of servant leader you are. Whether you seek to serve or to be served. If you are about God's glory or your own glory. This is why we must strive, in the Spirit's power, to do the little, forgotten, overlooked things that no one else wants to do, and do them with thankfulness and joy!

The love of Christ within us compels us to lead like this. To lead like Him. Let us remember each and every day that we GET to be pastors. It is a gift from God! Pastoral ministry is a challenge, yes, but it is also an absolute joy and privilege. May we never stop being amazed that God has given us the unique and special opportunity to shepherd His people. Cultivating humility in our hearts is the critical ingredient that will help us stay amazed and in awe of this glorious calling of which each of us is unworthy.

See the value of every person in the congregation.

Humble pastors don't play favorites or try to be the coolest show in town. Humble pastors want to love the things that Jesus loves—namely, people. Jesus loves every soul in your congregation. The popular, the unpopular. The rich, the poor. The extrovert, the introvert. Those who look like you and those who don't. These are God's people, redeemed by Christ, ordained by God to be precious souls that we oversee and care for. Every person in your congregation has value in the eyes of God. Do they have value in *your* eyes?

Choosing to fall in love with the flock God has entrusted to you as a pastor must increasingly take precedence over any fleshly desire you might have to lead some "cool" church filled with "cool," "influential" people. I have met many pastors who spend more time daydreaming about the congregation they wish they had than pouring into and loving well the congregation they do have—the congregation God, in His kind providence, put under their charge.

Fellow revitalizers, becoming the coolest or biggest church on the block cannot be the desire of our hearts. Our heart's cry must continually be, "God, I want to make a big deal about You, in the way You want me to, with the people You have called me to. I want to be a good shepherd, a humble servant to these sheep, because every one of them matters. Every person in this congregation is wonderfully made in Your image and needs Jesus. Every believer here is precious because he or she is Your child, deeply loved, chosen in Christ."

Listen deeply to understand others' viewpoints and perspectives.

"If one gives an answer before he hears, it is his folly and shame."
- Proverbs 18:13

How fitting these words from Proverbs 18 are for a revitalization pastor! When you begin to lead a dying or declining church, serving your people through careful, thoughtful, deep listening is one of the greatest, most important gifts you can give. Attentive listening is a very tangible way to display humility.

Can you think of a time when you sat down to talk with a pastor or leader of some kind, and it was very obvious that he or she was not listening to you? This pastor or leader was not engaged with you or in tune with what you were saying. Perhaps he or she seemed distracted, annoyed, or antsy as you tried to communicate. How did that make you feel? If you are like me, in those situations the last thing I feel is cared for. In fact, it makes me feel the opposite. It is hurtful and doesn't make me want to visit with that individual again anytime soon.

Of course, you can probably also think of times in which pastors or other leaders did listen actively to you. They were truly present in your conversation. You felt like they truly cared about what you had to say. You felt affirmed. Even if they didn't completely agree with your view or perspective, you felt loved and respected.

What kind of listener will you be, pastor? As we listen attentively to others, we communicate that we truly do care and that we don't believe we have all the answers. This is why we should make every effort to grow as good question askers. Asking good questions is significant in building relationships of trust and understanding with those in a congregation. These simple acts of giving others our focused attention show concern and compassion to people. And they are especially critical for those who have, for years, sacrificially given their lives and resources to keep this declining church afloat.

Look for ways to improve your leadership.

Pastors should always be growing as leaders. Very few pastors I have met would disagree with this statement. When it comes down to it, however, it is rare to find a pastor who is truly doing what it takes to be stretched and constantly growing in his leadership. Clearly, maturing as a leader doesn't just happen. One doesn't just drift into becoming a strong leader of others. It takes hunger, humility, teachability, and ongoing intentionality.

One of the key characteristics of an effective revitalizer is his ability to lead as a visionary shepherd. When we step inside a struggling church, it might be made up of only thirty or forty sweet folks who need us to love them, feed them, encourage them, and shepherd them well. At the same time, they need to be led with fresh vision and passion! We need to bring hope and vision for what God can do in and through this church. We must help them see and believe that God is not done with them!

The way this will happen most effectively over time is if we are growing as visionary leaders ourselves. We cannot take people where we haven't been. We can't give what we don't have.

Let me encourage you to be learning from other strong, gifted leaders and churches that have been through the same types of leadership challenges your congregation is facing. Pursue great leaders! Read their books. Listen to their teachings. Try to connect with them so you can ask a handful of good questions, and then soak up their wisdom. Then, by God's grace and wisdom, seek to put into practice some of what you learn.

You never "arrive" in leadership. Be relentless in your learning and growth as a leader.

Don't overreact when errors are made or ministry ideas and programs fall flat.

The most effective revitalizers I know are willing to try stuff and fail. In other words, they are willing to dream up and implement new ministry ideas, programs, and events, knowing that sometimes they will fall flat. The thing is, when there is failure, these leaders don't give up, and they don't let discouragement overtake them. Nor do they allow discouragement to overtake others. No, these leaders get back up, they help everyone else get back up, and they begin dreaming about trying something else for the Lord!

Sometimes the things we try in ministry simply don't work the way we thought they would. Oftentimes, we flat-out fail. This happens to every one of us. Your people need to know that this is normal. They need to know from watching your response that it is truly okay to try something new and fail. If you freak out every time someone in your congregation tries something that doesn't work, over time you will create an environment of fear in which no one will want to use their gifts. Your people will begin to shrink back out of worry or dread of letting you and others down. Do you know where this inevitably leads for pastors? It leads to our doing everything by ourselves. Nothing is less fun and less effective than this. More than that, we will hinder our people from using the very passions and spiritual gifts the Lord Himself has given them to use for His purposes.

This is why you must lead your church to become a culture of grace. A culture of grace says, "Hey, let's give it a shot. If it doesn't work, it's okay!" Grace brings a sense of freedom and joy, which also helps create an environment in which people come alive using their gifts in ministry. This mindset of grace also helps create momentum for growth in your church.

Grace is the key. Grace is a catalyst for greater faith and trust within a congregation. And grace-filled leaders are humble leaders. They are individuals who have been transformed by the grace of Jesus in their own lives, and now this grace overflows into how they humbly love and lead others. You see, a humble heart allows you as a leader to say and believe, "My identity is not based on the perfection of the programs and events in our church. My identity is in Jesus. I don't need to overreact when things don't go as planned. I can extend grace to people in the same way that Jesus has extended so much grace to me." This is where joy in ministry is found! This is where you find the strength and sustainability for the long haul in ministry. It all begins with a heart posture of humility.

Grow in gentleness and strength.

There's a tension that naturally exists between being strong and being gentle. It's like a soldier who battles a strong enemy in combat and yet speaks softly to a refugee child. Or, a shepherd who beats back a wolf and yet also cradles a little lamb. We want to be strong leaders—not strong in our own strength, but strong in the Lord. We want to be courageous. We want to take risks for God and His glory. But at the same time, we must be marked by gentleness. Gentleness is one of the prerequisites of a biblical pastor (1 Timothy 3:3). Gentleness means that as we lead and as we shepherd, our congregation knows that we are approachable, kindhearted, and teachable. This kind of gentleness is rooted in humility before God and others.

Think about a mother's tenderness toward her children. Paul compares his love and care for the believers in Thessalonica to that of a mother to her children. We read in 1 Thessalonians 2:7-8,

> But we were gentle among you, like a nursing mother taking care of her own children. So, being affectionately desirous of you, we were ready to share with you not only the gospel of God but also our own selves, because you had become very dear to us.

This is how we should be with the sheep that God entrusts to us as pastor-shepherds. Not distant, but affectionate. Not complacent, but caring. Not harsh, but gentle. Gentleness should mark the leadership of a revitalization pastor, while at the same time, seeking to be strong in the strength the Lord alone provides.

Forgive quickly, remembering how the Lord has forgiven you.

"Be kind to one another, tenderhearted, forgiving one another, as God in Christ forgave you." - Ephesians 4:32

By God's grace, we must never lose sight of the cross in our lives and in our ministries. We must never forget the depths from which we have been saved by Jesus. We must never forget who we are in Him and who He is making us to be by His mercy and kindness alone. It is in understanding and believing more and more deeply these Gospel realities that we learn to forgive others as we have been forgiven by Christ. If we don't get this, we will often become grudge-holding, angry pastors and leaders. We will become bitter toward others. And this is a dark and dangerous place to be in both life and ministry.

The reality is, as revitalizers, we will be hurt by others. As much as we might not like it, the words and actions of others will at times wound us deeply. This is probably the biggest reason why so many pastors prematurely leave hard churches and difficult ministry contexts. So, what do we do about this? How do we respond to those who cause us great hurt and pain in church revitalization?

We must learn to forgive. By God's grace and power, we must learn to forgive people quickly, remembering how the Lord has forgiven us. Let me tell you why. If we aren't quick to forgive through the power of the Gospel, our hurt and pain will continue to grow and intensify within us. And, over time, it will prevent us from being able to love people well. We will become guarded and distant. We will lack intimacy with our congregation. We will stop trusting people, and they will stop trusting us. This is where a lack of forgiveness leads. What the Lord desires for each of us is this: He wants to help us become pastors and leaders who are gracious forgivers, growing deeper in our understanding and application of Gospel truth to our own hearts and minds.

Share the pulpit.

One of the things I love about our church is that we are blessed to have multiple individuals who are gifted to preach and teach God's Word. It was not always that way. In fact, in each of my first two years leading our struggling congregation, I remember preaching 49 out of 52 weeks, if my memory serves me right. Of course, when you are a very small, declining congregation, with one pastor, this is often the only option. I am truly grateful for our sweet congregation for so graciously sitting through my preaching week after week those first few years!

However, I was convinced then, just as I am now, that this model of having one pastor who preaches week in and week out, year in and year out, is not the wisest, healthiest, most biblical or sustainable model for a pastor or congregation that desires to grow in a healthy way over the long haul. So, though I love to preach, I knew I had to work hard to raise up other preachers to share the load. To help feed the flock, for the good of our people, the good of my family, the good of my soul, and ultimately for the glory of God.

While I continue to preach the majority of the time, it is not uncommon to see other pastors in the pulpit regularly at our church. This is by design. This is a conviction. If you have never been part of a congregation that shares the pulpit regularly between different preachers, let me briefly share ten reasons why I believe this is so important, not only for our church but for other congregations as well. Each of these plays a vital role in helping a pastor practice humility in their preaching ministry.

Reason #1: Jesus is the only Hero. This is huge. Any church that is built on one preacher is vulnerable to making that individual the hero, rather than Jesus. As Jared Wilson writes,

> Your church needs to know that it is the Bible properly taught that is their source of strength, not a particular man and only that man teaching it. This is the inner error in many video venue enterprises. Some will say the satellite would not be viable without the "celebrity" preacher preaching, in which case I think it could be argued that if it could not survive without a particular person's voice, it is not viable to begin with. (What happens if that pastor has a heart attack? Does every satellite shut down? Or do they just play old videos?)[1]

Sharing the pulpit on a regular basis, especially with other men who are also gifted in preaching, helps to keep a pastor humble. It helps to keep Jesus the hero.

Reason #2: Obedience to Scripture. Our congregation is now led by a plurality of pastors (i.e. elders) as taught in the New Testament. Not one. Multiple pastors. Some are paid, some are not. The Scripture teaches that it is the responsibility of all the pastors to preach and teach the Word of God to the flock, not just one individual (see Acts 6, 1 Tim. 3, Titus 1). This is a shared calling and responsibility. Sharing the pulpit in this way is about obedience to the Word and the way God wants His church to be led.

Reason #3: Setting the church up well for the future. A shared pulpit helps to assure that when the main preacher leaves or dies, the church remains steady and in a healthy spot to continue making disciples and feeding the flock well. As leaders, we must be looking to the future. Our philosophy and practice of preaching now will radically affect how our churches look and function 5, 10, 20 years from now.

Reason #4: Allows pastors to eat (spiritually speaking)! One of the great joys and blessings in my own spiritual life is sitting in the pew and feasting on the preached Word as it is delivered by one of our other pastors. I love having them preach to our congregation, but I also love being able to eat the Word they are preaching for my own soul. This is critical for the spiritual health of all of our pastors.

Reason #5: Family leadership and discipleship. It's a joy to sit with my wife and kids and hear the Word of God preached, together as a family. As I feast myself, I also love the opportunity to help my family feast. Helping my kids learn how to listen to a sermon effectively is part of my calling as their father and spiritual leader. I am only able to do this in a shared preaching model.

Reason #6: Needed time for other pastoral duties. Weeks where I am not preaching allow me to spend more focused attention on other vital aspects to my ministry and leadership including pastoral care, vision and strategy, mentoring, preaching and teaching prep, denominational responsibilities, etc. As our church has grown, these important areas of ministry need more of my time and attention as the lead pastor.

Reason #7: Pacing for long-term leadership health. Any preacher will tell you: Sermon prep is a joyful yet agonizing process. It takes incredible mental, emotional, spiritual, and physical energy every week. I typically spend around 20 hours preparing my sermons. Moreover, I preach hard for 40-45 minutes at three different services on a weekend. Over time, this will take a toll on a preacher if there is not a shared preaching model in place. I hope, by God's grace, to pastor and lead our church for many years to come. If this is to happen, I cannot crush myself by failing to share the pulpit. No one can do this alone for the long-term in a healthy way.

Reason #8: The blessing of hearing a variety of unified voices in the pulpit. A shared pulpit allows our congregation to be fed by different pastors, each with unique personalities and giftings. There is not one preacher who will connect with everyone in the same way in the same congregation. A shared preaching model helps our congregation to value and experience a variety of preachers, all committed to loving and shepherding God's people through the faithful, expositional preaching of God's Word.

Reason #9: Helping pastors grow as preachers. As with all members of our church body, we must intentionally seek to equip and develop pastors in using their gifts, specifically in the area of preaching and teaching. The last thing I (or our congregation for that matter) want to be complicit in is wasting the God-given preaching and teaching gifts of our pastors.

Reason #10: It stirs up in me (and our other preachers) fresh passion and joy to preach. I have found that sharing the pulpit allows the Holy Spirit to refresh my heart and my mind on weeks I am not preaching. When I have a week or two off from preaching, I have time to remember why this calling to preach is so important and what a joy and privilege it is to feed God's people from His Word! This always spurs me on toward renewed zeal, joy, and excitement to get back in the pulpit and swing for the fences for God's glory and the good of His people!

As pastors and leaders in declining churches, we must highly value the preaching of God's Word. We must take it seriously. We must desire to feed our people really well from the pulpit each and every weekend, by God's grace and the power of His Holy Spirit. For us to do this in a long haul, sustainable manner, a shared, team preaching model must be both a conviction and intentional practice for us.

Now, while this may not be a possibility at the moment, in light of the size and health of your current congregation, in time it will be. As the Lord revitalizes your church, bringing new life and fresh vision to your people, you must begin planning ahead now for a team preaching model. To assist you in this, I have a written the book, *Who will Preach?: Raising Up Shepherd Preachers in Your Church* to help you begin to intentionally raise up preachers in your church. Over time, developing other preachers will be one of the greatest gifts you can give to your church. It is also one of the wisest, most humble and Christ-like ways you can lead your family and your congregation. Remember, this is not "your" pulpit or "my" pulpit we are talking about. This is not the pulpit of any one pastor. This is the pulpit of one Savior. This is Jesus' pulpit. May His Name alone be made famous from it.

Practice team leadership and decision-making.

The best kind of leadership over time involves team decision-making. This takes humility on the part of the leader. The Scriptures provide the blueprint for a plurality of pastors in the local church. Because this model requires interaction with other leaders, team leadership mandates that each member humbles himself before the other members. No one person will get his way all the time because each team member is a part of the whole. This is a good thing! Team leadership helps to expose blind spots, as well as underdeveloped ideas and strategies, which we all have when left to make decisions on our own. Decision-making, as a team, is wisdom.

It should be a goal of ours to build a team-oriented culture in our entire church. Everything that we do—from children's ministry, to student ministry, to worship ministry, to deacon ministry, to pastoral ministry and care—should be led by teams of leaders. This is wise and God-honoring on so many levels. It also will produce the greatest ministry fruit over the long haul. However, for this to happen, the lead pastor will have to set the tone by prioritizing and valuing humble, team leadership.

Intentionally develop and deploy other leaders.

How will you develop and deploy leaders in your ministry? Do you have a plan? Have you thought through a clear strategy? Leadership development is crucial in every area of ministry in our churches. The question is, as pastors, are we secure enough in our calling to develop and deploy other leaders? Raising up and empowering others to lead takes humility.

Prideful pastors who love to build their own platform and make a name for themselves do not effectively develop and deploy other leaders. Why? Because others might get the praise. Others might steal "their glory." It takes the spotlight off of them. Sadly, this mindset poisons many pastors and leaders in the church. It's the opposite of what Christ wants in His leaders.

Humble pastors say, "God's Word is clear. I have been called to develop other people and to deploy them to use their gifts in ministry—to serve our community, to lead in music, to care for kids and teenagers, to plant churches, to minister to the poor. However it might look, my job is not to hinder the ministry of others, but to empower them. To help and encourage them. And it is my joy to do so!"

Embrace uncertainty and trust the Lord in the midst of it.

In Proverbs 3:5-8, we are reminded of the wonderful, comforting truth that we are to trust the Lord in all things, even when things don't make sense to us.

> Trust in the LORD with all your heart, and do not lean on your own understanding. In all your ways acknowledge him, and he will make straight your paths. Be not wise in your own eyes; fear the LORD, and turn away from evil. It will be healing to your flesh and refreshment to your bones.

Uncertainty is a given in ministry. As leaders, we need to be prepared to trust in the Lord's sovereignty and care, fully knowing that He is in control. We can be confident that even though things might not make sense to us at a given moment, they make perfect sense to God. This is where our theology is so important. If we don't believe in a big God who is sovereign and in control of even the crazy things that happen in our lives and churches, we will become hopeless. We will become discouraged. We may want to give up ministry altogether.

Uncertainty is a part of life in a fallen world. As we choose to trust the Lord and put our faith in Him, we show our congregations that even in the midst of uncertainty, God is in control and can be completely trusted to provide for everything we need, both individually and collectively. We want to show our people that this is His church. Jesus bought us with His own blood. As His children, then, we are secure in His love and care forever! The Lord has brought His people through tough times before, and He will be faithful to do it again. This is the posture of a humble, faith-filled pastor.

HOW TO CULTIVATE HUMILITY IN YOUR HEART

While we have considered several practical ways revitalization pastors ought to live out and model humility in their leadership, I want to close this chapter by highlighting some strategies for helping each of us weaken pride and cultivate humility in our own hearts first. The bottom line is that if we are going to practice humble, Christ-like leadership over the long haul, we must pursue growth in the following areas. May these practical suggestions encourage you in your journey to become the kind of humble pastor and leader people don't simply "have to" follow but "want to" follow![2]

Begin your day by acknowledging your dependence upon God and your need for God.

How do you begin your day? Every one of us has some kind of routine, whether it is a good one or a bad one! Let me encourage you to form a possibly new routine when you wake up each morning. Begin your day by acknowledging your dependence upon God and your need for God. Here is what we know: Sin—especially the sin of pride—is active, not passive. Sin doesn't wake up tired. So, we must go on the offensive from the moment we wake up. We must choose to submit to God and His Spirit first thing each morning. We must look to Him for strength from the moment we wake up to the moment we go to bed. This daily acknowledgement of our need for God will help grow in us a posture and attitude of humility before the Lord and others.

Reflect on the wonder of the cross.

To paraphrase John Owen, if our affections are captivated by the cross of Christ, there will be no room for sin. How often do we stop and simply stand amazed at the cross? How often do we take the time to meditate on key passages dealing with the work of Christ on the cross on our behalf? We *must* do this! This must become a daily discipline if we are to grow as Gospel-centered Christians and Gospel-centered pastors. To reflect on the wonder of the cross. To stand amazed at His love and sacrifice for sinners like us. To celebrate these wonderful Gospel realities! To sing songs of praise for Christ's amazing grace and mercy! Reflecting on the wonder of the cross helps keep us humble.

Take responsibility for your sin...stop blaming others.

How easy it is to justify our sin or to pass the blame of our sin onto others! Some of us live our entire lives this way, and we are miserable because of it. Both freedom and joy in the Lord come with taking responsibility for our sin. This is critical if we are to have a healthy, growing, vibrant relationship with God.

As we read in 1 John 1:9, "If we confess our sins, he is faithful and just and will forgive us our sins and purify us from all unrighteousness." Refusing to be honest about our sin before God will absolutely suck the life out of our relationship with Him.

This is just as true in our relationships with others—with our spouse, our kids, our friends, our bosses and co-workers, etc. We must be quick to own where we fall short and then quickly ask for forgiveness. It takes humility to say to someone, "Please forgive me for _____." Yet, this attitude is essential to living a life marked by genuine humility.

Don't be so sure you're right all the time...be teachable.

I have news for you: There are actually people in the world who know more than you and I do. More than that, there are actually people in the world who are far more discerning than you and I are. Humility helps us to recognize that we don't know it all! Humility causes us to be quick to listen, slow to speak, and eager to learn from others much wiser than us. Humility helps us to be easily edified. How I pray that we will be the kinds of pastors—the kinds of Christians—who are easily edified as a result of a humble, teachable heart.

I love how Justin Taylor puts it:

> Wouldn't it be great if those who knew us best could honestly say, "It is **so** easy to edify him. It doesn't take much. It doesn't need to be the best sermon ever preached or the most excellent song ever composed or the most powerful book ever written or the most theologically eloquent statement ever uttered. Just the simplest truth was enough to refresh his heart in Christ."[3]

May this become our prayer—that the Lord would help us to be easily taught and, as a result, easily edified as He grows us in humility.

Ask for prayer for areas of weakness and temptation.

It's humbling to ask others to pray for us because then we're admitting that we are weak. And we want everyone to think we're strong. The truth is we really are weak. Naming this reality should actually be liberating for us (and for those around us). You and I desperately need the encouragement and prayers of our brothers and sisters in Christ far more than we even realize. In asking for prayer in areas of weakness and temptation, we are showing those whom we lead that we need the Gospel of grace just as much as anyone else. Asking for prayer allows us to be honest and genuine and humble with others. It also allows us to point others to Christ and to boast in Him alone in the midst of our weaknesses. As the Apostle Paul writes, describing his battle with a thorn in his flesh (2 Corinthians 12:9-10),

> But he said to me, "My grace is sufficient for you, for my power is made perfect in weakness." Therefore I will boast all the more gladly of my weaknesses, so that the power of Christ may rest upon me. For the sake of Christ, then, I am content with weaknesses, insults, hardships, persecutions, and calamities. For when I am weak, then I am strong.

May this same attitude concerning the Lord's strength in our weakness mark our lives on a daily basis.

Get good sleep.

Most of us are "on the go" all the time. We find it difficult to slow down and actually rest. This constant "going" often negatively impacts our sleep patterns. One of the things I have learned over the years in ministry is just how important good sleep is for our minds, our bodies, and our souls. Good sleep cannot be optional for those of us who desire to pastor faithfully over the long haul.

We must receive the gift of sleep from God and acknowledge His purpose for sleep. The fact that we need rest and sleep should be a constant reminder that we are not God. It should be an indication of just how weak and needy we are. When we don't get good sleep for days at a time, we get cranky and can't focus. Every time we lay our head on that pillow, it should cause us to pray, "Lord, you are God and I am not. Thank you that I can just rest in your presence tonight. Jesus, help me to sleep well. Renew me. Because I am so dependent on you." Good sleep reminds us of our dependence on the Lord. Good sleep helps to cultivate humility in our hearts.

Study God.

Theology is transformative because it helps us more accurately understand ourselves, while enlarging and clarifying our understanding of God. If you look at some of the godliest pastors throughout the history of the Church, you understand that they were theologians. But not just any kind of theologian.

They were theologians who worshipped God with increasing zeal and passion as a result of their theology!

Studying theology should not just be a means of filling our minds with knowledge. It should fuel the affections of our hearts as we grow more and more amazed by the nature and character of God and by His majesty over all things. It should drive us to our knees in worship. This is why, in our preaching, we want to be both Word-driven and doctrinal at the same time. We want to show people God for who He really is, as revealed in Scripture, that they might live for the glory and praise of His name. That is what preaching is. If we instead communicate to our parishioners, *"It's all about you!"* we have missed the primary point of preaching, which is to exalt God and worship Him.

Laugh at yourself!

Proud men cannot laugh at themselves. Make sure you can! We can't take ourselves too seriously. The longer we work in ministry, the more apparent this becomes. If people cannot poke fun at us, then there is something seriously wrong. We have got to be comfortable with folks poking fun at us. We have to be more than okay—and not take it personally—when goofy things happen in the church. Ask God to help you grow in the ability to laugh at yourself while letting others laugh at you too! Leaders who can laugh at themselves are the types of leaders with whom people feel safe.

Identify evidences of God's grace in others through intentional encouragement.

Open your eyes to see God's amazing work in the lives of others. Don't focus on others' failures. As leaders, are we quick to criticize, or are we quick to encourage? That's an important question. If we are quick to criticize, quick to be negative, or quick to be cynical, this is evidence of a heart that is unhealthy. There is pride and insecurity in there. Over time, this will hurt people. We need to be willing to do our own heart work first before our harshness causes great damage not only to our ministries, but to our families and our churches.

There is so much good that is happening in people's lives! There is so much good that is happening in our churches! Do we see it? Are we looking for it? The best leaders see the great things God is doing and points them out for all to see. In doing this, we get to show God off and give Him glory. Humility fuels the heart of those who love to identify and illuminate the work of God's grace in the lives of others. This is called encouragement! Dying churches need pastors who encourage others with great joy and intentionality.

Grow in and practice self-awareness.

How well do you know yourself? Growing in self-awareness is critical if we desire to be effective leaders and revitalizers. This involves knowing accurately how you are gifted and how you are *not* gifted. Different people are given different gifts by God. This is a good and beautiful thing! Be honest about your strengths and weaknesses and surround yourself with those who complement your gifting. Don't feel threatened by those who are more gifted than you. This is good for your heart. This type of humble honesty helps to keep your pride in check and protects others from putting you on a pedestal, where you certainly don't belong.

Practice thankfulness.

Are you a thankful person? What would those closest to you say? Whether or not we always realize it, we have so much reason to give thanks to the Lord. Everything we have is a gift from Him! We also have much reason to show thankfulness to others. As we shepherd God's people and seek to lead a struggling congregation back to health, we must express radical, continual thankfulness and gratitude to others.

Expressing thankfulness to those you lead will not only encourage them, it will show them in a tangible way that you love them and love being their pastor. This love will win their hearts over time, which is absolutely critical in church revitalization. As you thank the Lord for who He is and all He has done, form the habit of regularly telling your people that you are thankful for them too. Humble revitalizers are thankful leaders.

Invite correction in your own life.

As leaders, we ought to increasingly desire correction in our lives. To increasingly accept the nuggets of truth that come with correction, no matter the source. Be quick to receive feedback. In fact, ask for it. As painful as it may be, we must be proactive in this. If we have done something wrong, let us not be too proud to humbly name it. If we have hurt another person, let us be quick to go to that person and ask, *"How could I have handled this better?"* This is a heart growing in humility, by the grace of God. Moreover, this is the kind of leader and pastor those in a dying or declining church will come to love and trust.

HUMILITY IS FOUNDATIONAL

The Lord loves humility in His people. In fact, humility is the foundation not only of all faithful Christian leadership, but of all faithful Christian living. For this reason, humility is crucial in the heart and leadership of a revitalization pastor. Of course, a problem is this: Not only do we by nature rebel from humility, we live in a world that does not value humility. At times, even churches do not value humility. Yet the Lord does. The Lord loves humility in His people! By His grace, may we seek to love and shepherd the tired, hurting, hungry sheep the Lord has entrusted to our care. And may we do it with Christ-like humility, daily remembering, "God opposes the proud but gives grace to the humble" (James 4:6).

FOR FURTHER REFLECTION

JOURNAL / DISCUSSION

1. Take a minute to reflect on your life and your heart – would you say that you are growing in humility? Would the people around you say that you are humble? Why or why not?

2. How have you seen a lack of humility damage yourself or others close to you in ministry? What are some specific examples?

3. Which of the marks of humble revitalizers are the biggest challenge for you? Why is this?

4. What we say tells a lot about what's in our heart – when you introduce yourself and get to know someone, how do you talk about yourself? Do you make yourself the main character or God? Take a minute to write out an introduction of yourself that reflects a humble heart.

5. Reflect back on your leadership for the last month (at home, at work, in ministry) – have you been intentional about giving those around you opportunities to lead and giving them credit or are you looking for the spotlight moment to draw attention to yourself? What are ways that you can step to the side and help others to shine in their leadership today?

6. When you think of being a servant leader, are there tasks that you would say you won't do? Why or why not? What does that say about your heart? As you go through your day today, watch for obscure and unnoticeable ways to serve...and do those tasks without telling anyone or asking for credit. Take note of how this made you feel.

7. Keeping in mind the suggestions in this chapter for cultivating humility, which of these would you like to be more intentional about integrating into your life and relationship with God?

8. Are you aware of your weaknesses and seeking to grow in them? Who are two people in your life to help you see yourself as you are so that false senses of pride don't sneak in?

PRAY

-   Take few minutes to confess your pride to the Lord and ask for forgiveness. Ask Him to examine your heart and to remove the seeds of pride within. Pray that God would open your eyes to see yourself as you truly are and that He would grow you in humility.

-   Pray that God would be seen more in your ministry than you are and that He and His glory would continue to be your greatest passion in life and ministry.

> *"Do nothing from selfish ambition or conceit, but in humility count others more significant than yourselves. Let each of you look not only to his own interests, but also to the interests of others."*
>
> *- Philippians 2:3-4*

CHAPTER 2

PATIENCE

THE WISDOM OF GODLY LEADERSHIP

"Rejoice in hope, be patient in tribulation, be constant in prayer."
- Romans 12:12

Patience is a really good thing. I don't know about you, but I love being around patient people. I love hanging out with those who don't get irritated easily by the everyday annoyances of life or overreact to circumstances that are out of their control. There is a calming presence that patient people have about them. I love it.

But there's a problem.

Practicing patience is something most of us are not very good at. It is also something we rarely celebrate or value in our culture. We live in a day and age in which we can fly anywhere in the world, download the newest music, record all kinds of TV shows or movies, and quite literally get ahold of almost anyone, anywhere in the world, whenever we want. As far as the world is concerned, what is the point of pursuing patience in our lives? It seems foolish!

Albert Mohler writes,

> Most of us recognize that patience is one of the cardinal Christian virtues—we're just in no hurry to obtain it. Others just define patience as a delay in getting what we want. As Margaret Thatcher once famously remarked: "I am extraordinarily patient, provided I get my own way in the end." In today's fast-paced society and self-centered culture, patience is quickly disappearing, even among Christians.[4]

Likewise, Sam Storms rightly notes,

> No one comes by patience naturally. No one instinctively responds to adversity and interruptions without at least some measure of irritation and anger. No one encounters opposition to one's plans without some degree of agitation and frustration. Patience, to put it simply, is counter-intuitive. It is not something with which we are born. It is, instead, a work of God's grace in the human heart, a fruit of the Holy Spirit in our lives.[5]

When it comes to the work of church revitalization, patience is a fruit that we as pastors desperately need the Holy Spirit to grow in us. Stepping into a struggling church, we will immediately find ourselves loving very tired—probably even burned out and deeply discouraged—folks. Moreover, we will need to be constantly discerning how best to lead within the framework of old systems, structures, and traditions that have shaped the culture of this church for many, many years. To rightly love and lead in a context like this, we will need patience that can only come from the Lord Himself.

We must remember that healthy change takes patience because healthy change takes time. Obviously, congregations are made up of individuals. And for change to happen in an entire congregation, change must take place in each of the lives that make up the congregation. This doesn't happen overnight. It almost always takes a great deal of time.

Patience is needed to help people experience true, Gospel change in their lives. I just recently visited with a man who has been a pastor in the same church for many years. Almost every week, for eighteen years straight, he has intentionally met with and poured his life into one particular young man in his church. For most of these years, there has been seemingly very little fruit, which has led to seasons of great discouragement for my pastor friend. However, just recently, after eighteen years, my friend shared how God has begun to do unbelievable things in this young man's life, though he isn't so young anymore! In our time together, I could tell my friend was deeply encouraged and thankful for the Lord's faithfulness after all of these years. I share this because it is a great example of the kind of pastoral patience we must develop as church revitalizers if we are to be effective shepherds of God's people through the ups and downs that come over the years in ministry.

WHAT IS BIBLICAL PATIENCE?

To be honest, left to ourselves and our own strength, I have very little hope of any of us ever becoming truly patient pastors and leaders. I just don't. But the good news is that the Lord has not called us to grow in patience by ourselves, on our own, apart from Him. Thankfully, the opposite is true. The Holy Spirit is working in us daily, transforming us and conforming us more to the image and character of Christ.

Paul writes about the different types of "fruit" that the Holy Spirit is producing and developing in God's people: "But the fruit of the Spirit is love, joy, peace, patience, kindness, goodness, faithfulness, gentleness, self-control..." (Galatians 5:22-23). The Holy Spirit is producing the characteristics of Christ within us. One of these is patience. Christ-like patience.

The word for "patience" comes from the Greek word, μακροθυμία *(makrothumia)*. There is a lot of meaning packed into this Greek word. It is a term that combines two different words. *Makros* is defined as "long or far," and *thumos* means "anger or wrath." When we put these two words together, we quite literally come up with "long-anger." The opposite is "short-anger" or "short-temper." If someone is short-tempered, they are a very impatient person. *Makrothumia* is speaking of someone who is the opposite of this. They are long-tempered. In other words, they display a Spirit-empowered patience that is honoring to the Lord and loving toward others.

Clearly, being an impatient leader is out of step with the Spirit's desired work in our lives. Practically speaking, if we are not long-tempered, our leadership efforts in church revitalization will become very frustrating and ineffective. As we seek to love and shepherd the people in our congregation, our lack of patience will result in anger and bitterness toward the very sheep God has entrusted us to love and care for. The very sheep Jesus died to save.

Living out biblical patience takes a lot of humility and a lot of love. It takes the power of the Holy Spirit. The truth is, we will be ministering to all different kinds of people, some of whom are very difficult and trying of our patience. While we will at times be tempted, in our flesh, to lash out at them in anger or ask them to leave our church and go worship elsewhere, the Lord has called us to these sheep. Our patience will be tested, no question. But the good news is that God promises to equip us and empower us to grow into the long-suffering, loving leaders He wants us to be. Let's think through some of the different types of people we must learn to lead with patience.

SPECIFIC TYPES OF PEOPLE
WE MUST LEARN TO LEAD WITH PATIENCE

#1. Those who Resist and Even Oppose Change

We should be prepared for the reality that there will be individuals in our congregations who will resist and oppose change of all kinds, big or small. And they will do this for a variety of reasons. Some are legitimate reasons; many are not. Either way, change that is sure to come will be hard for many people. We must be ready for this.

For some, change is difficult because they have a deeply rooted history with the church. They have been there for years, and many of their closest friends and sweetest life memories have been connected to their church. The thought of things changing is unsettling for them. It feels to them as though they are losing part of who they are. Others have helped to hold this declining church together for years both financially and through their committed leadership. When families began to leave the church in order to attend other, more healthy congregations, these faithful men and women hung in there. They have been faithful to this church when few others were. As a result, they are skeptical of changes because they are skeptical that those leading them will be around for the long haul. Still, others feel that changes in the church will result in the older segment of the congregation being forgotten and left behind, perhaps discarded, in lieu of a younger congregation. They worry that as the church moves into the future, they will forget about the past.

The bottom line is that there will be those in our church who will resist change for many different reasons. We must acknowledge this and seek to wisely and patiently work to win the hearts of these individuals, to earn their trust as we carefully move forward with changes. We must humbly listen to them, spend time with them, and value them as sheep who need a caring shepherd to lead them well.

#2. Those who are Slow to Learn

We must be patient with those who are slow to learn. Here is what I mean: We are going into churches where the Bible has most likely not been taught very well for a long time. There are biblical and doctrinal truths that you would think those who have been part of this church for many years should have grasped, understood, and applied to their lives by now. We may wonder, *"Why don't these people get it? Why don't they know more about the Gospel, the Bible, and living on mission than they do?"* Again, we cannot expect sheep who have not been fed and shepherded well for years to be healthy, well-nurtured disciples. Many of these individuals are hungry for the Word, but they have been given milk for so long that they have forgotten how to ingest solid teaching. They have been stunted in their spiritual growth. They have become like a fig tree that cannot produce fruit. Jesus speaks to this in Luke 13:6-9,

> And he told this parable: "A man had a fig tree planted in his vineyard, and he came seeking fruit on it and found none. And he said to the vinedresser, 'Look, for three years now I have come

seeking fruit on this fig tree, and I find none. Cut it down. Why should it use up the ground?' And he answered him, 'Sir, let it alone this year also, until I dig around it and put on manure. Then if it should bear fruit next year, well and good; but if not, you can cut it down.'"

Our job is to help God's people grow and mature. May we patiently dig around their roots and fertilize their hearts and minds so they can draw in nutrient-rich teaching. This will allow them to flourish and produce good fruit!

#3. Those who are Weak in the Faith

"Now faith is the assurance of things hoped for, the conviction of things not seen." - Hebrews 11:1

As we journey into a church revitalization context, we are going to find people from various walks of life. Many of them have been beaten down and have grown weary of the battle. They will have doubts about whether or not God actually cares—not only for them personally, but for their church. We are going to be spending a lot of time loving these people—teaching the Scriptures to them, encouraging them, praying for them, and discipling them.

There could very well be others who are wrestling with serious questions about the character and even existence of God. Some of these individuals are humble and desire to learn. However, there could also be others who initially are not interested in learning, but rather wish to quarrel. It will be easy to become impatient with these people, and yet what we need to show them is deep love, much grace, and great patience. God, in His timing, is at work in them. Remember, He is working on them just like He is working on us. Clearly, it isn't anger and wrath that changes hearts; it is grace and kindness. This is the beautiful truth of the gracious Gospel that has changed each one of us. As Paul teaches in Romans 2:4, it is God's kindness that leads us to repentance. May we also share the Lord's kindness with those who are weak in faith.

#4. Those who are Quick to Complain and Slow to Encourage

Criticism is part of the territory when it comes to pastoral ministry. While not fun, it is a reality. We are going to have those in our congregations who are very quick to criticize, very quick to complain about all kinds of things, but very slow to encourage. This is particularly true in the early stages of a revitalization. Again, we must be ready for this. In the face of being criticized and in the face of complaints, we must humble ourselves and seek to intentionally pursue our critics with love and grace. We must be willing to hear their complaints and be willing to learn, even if we don't completely agree. Paul puts it this way,

> And the Lord's servant must not be quarrelsome but kind to everyone, able to teach, patiently enduring evil, correcting his opponents with gentleness. God may perhaps grant them repentance leading to a knowledge of the truth, and they may come to their senses and escape from the snare of the devil, after being captured by him to do his will. - 2 Timothy 2:24-26

Even if we don't always agree with our critics' beliefs, perceptions, and reasoning, we would be wise to listen to them thoughtfully and carefully in order to understand them better. Whether we like it or not, these critics are typically an integral part of our church family. Do not ignore them! There could very well be deeper heart issues that you as their pastor can help them address and deal with before their bitterness spreads like a disease to the entire church.

Lean into your critics. Don't run from them. Trust the Lord to give you His strength, courage, wisdom, and patience in ministering to them.

#5. Those who are Forgetful or "Flaky" in Their Responsibilities

Part of leadership development is training people to be mature in their understanding of responsibility. To help them take ownership of those things we have entrusted them with or entrusted them to do. We will have congregants who tend to be "flaky" or forgetful, which can be very frustrating as a leader. But guess what? This is simply the reality in every church. While some in our congregation will be punctual, detail-oriented, and faithful to follow through with any and every ministry commitment they make, there will be plenty of others who are marked by the opposite of these things. This should not take us by surprise. If we are going to care for each of these different types of people, and if we are going to develop different types of leaders, we must be prepared and ready to show great patience and grace toward those who are forgetful or flake out in their responsibilities.

Here are a couple of passages to consider on this topic:

> "And we urge you, brothers, admonish the idle, encourage the fainthearted, help the weak, be patient with them all." - 1 Thessalonians 5:14

Paul, when he was writing this, understood that within the body of Christ there will be all kinds of people, including the idle, the fainthearted, and the weak. We are called to be patient with them all.

In 2 Timothy 4:2, Paul writes to Timothy, a young pastor whom he had mentored,

> "Preach the word; be ready in season and out of season; reprove, rebuke, and exhort, with complete patience and teaching."

As we instruct people, as we preach the Word and disciple them, all of this must be undergirded with a deep sense and practice of godly, Spirit-empowered patience in our leadership.

9 REASONS WHY REVITALIZERS MUST PRACTICE PATIENCE

In light of the five different types of folks listed above, let's consider nine reasons why we as revitalizers must practice patience in order to be the best leaders and shepherds we can be for God's people.

#1. People process change at different rates of speed.

Again, Paul writes in 1 Thessalonians 5:14, "And we urge you, brothers, admonish the idle, encourage the fainthearted, help the weak, **be patient** with them all" (emphasis mine).

This is something every pastor should think about regularly. In each of our churches, we will have a mix of people who respond differently to change. We will have individuals who love change and are on board with new changes very quickly. We will have others who don't like change at all, and it will take much longer to get them on board. Patience is one of the key ingredients that helps us bring unity in the body and lead change effectively within a congregation.

Yet, as vital as patience is, this is one of the primary areas in which many revitalizers fail in their leadership. It is very common for a new revitalization pastor to come into a declining church with a big, exciting vision, but then move far too quickly in seeking to carry out that vision. As a result, people fail to get on board with the new pastor and what he wants to do. Trust is lost, people are hurt, and momentum is thwarted. All too often, these kinds of rough-shot decisions and actions end up either leading to that pastor's being fired or serving as the catalyst for a heartbreaking church split. Impatience as a pastor never leads to anywhere good. This is particularly true when helping a struggling church get turned around.

#2. Developing a leadership culture in the church takes time and a great deal of patience.

People develop at *their* own speed, not ours. Most visionary leaders desire to see people develop quickly. We want to see people grow and mature into strong leaders in our time frame, which is a fast one! Typically, however, this kind of growth and maturity is slow. It happens over a long period of time. We must be mindful of this! Whether it is in children's ministry, small group ministry, music ministry, or on the greeting team, every area of ministry in our church must work patiently to develop leaders, knowing that it takes time.

Creating a leadership culture in your church will take a great deal of intentionality. It will take a great deal of patience too. You must be content with this reality. Individuals will grow into leaders at different rates. The most effective revitalizers understand this and take the time needed to develop leaders the right way—over time.

#3. Many conflicts can be avoided when we avoid jumping to conclusions and taking unwise actions.

Have you ever jumped to false conclusions about a person or a situation before gathering all the facts? I know I have. And it can be disastrous! As revitalizers, when conflict or tension arises between individuals or ministry team members in the church, we must patiently understand the situation before jumping to conclusions. When conflict resolution is needed, we must be willing to take sufficient time to truly understand the situation and establish the facts before rushing to judgment and taking action that could be unwise and damaging.

All too often in our impatience to obtain conflict resolution, we deal with things too quickly, which may very well create a larger conflict. This does not have to happen. Many conflicts can be avoided by rightly assessing the situation and proceeding slowly with all of the facts clearly understood. Take your time. Work to understand the facts. This is wisdom.

#4. Patience helps us to be better listeners.

Great leaders tend to be great listeners. As revitalizers, we want to hear the hearts and listen to the stories of those who have been part of this declining church for years, perhaps even decades. Consider three things we as leaders must regularly remind ourselves about good listening:

1. We must intentionally ask good questions. Are we good question askers? Are we thoughtful question askers? Are we regularly and intentionally asking important questions to different types of people in our churches, including those who have been there for a long time?

2. **We must listen carefully to the answers people give.** This means we must listen thoughtfully and patiently. We want to hear people share stories from their lives. We want to hear stories from the congregation's history. We want to hear individual's thoughts and opinions and perspectives. The information gathered after careful listening should shape how we lead and shepherd those in this congregation.

3. **We must take appropriate action or inaction from what we hear.** When I stop and think about it, every revitalizer I know who has been effective in leading healthy change in a declining church is an individual who asks great questions, is a great listener, and then is a wise action, or inaction, taker. Patience is the key ingredient in each of these.

#5. Impatience often causes leaders to make bad leadership decisions that can often hurt the church.

Most of the time, we need to be slow leaders. Not lazy. Not apathetic. Not passionless. Slow. Slowness is wise. Slowness is unifying. Slowness allows everybody to get on the bus and move forward together. If we make decisions too quickly, oftentimes it will come back to bite us. People get hurt. The church gets hurt. Messes are created that can be very difficult to clean up. Remember, speed is not always a good thing, especially when revitalizing a church.

#6. Leading with patience allows revitalizers to build support in the church.

Patience gives us time to earn trust. And we must do all that we can to earn trust. If we don't build trust with the congregation, those in our churches will not follow our leadership. They will question our motives. They will second-guess our love and encouragement toward them.

Listen, if our people don't believe that we genuinely care about them, the last thing they will ever do is give their lives to the vision we want to bring to the church. Leading with patience is critical if we are going to get the support and the backing that we need to guide this congregation into a healthy and fruitful future.

#7. Leading with patience can help us manage stress in the church and in our own lives.

Church revitalization can bring a lot of stress. We need to learn from the beginning how to manage it in our personal lives and also in the church. If we are stressed out all the time, we shouldn't be surprised when those we are leading get stressed out as well. Spirit-empowered patience is often the antidote to this kind of stress, anxiety, and worry.

Here's a tip in preventing stress: Know the "triggers" that cause you to grow impatient with others. In other words, what makes you snap? Know well these triggers and the circumstances leading up to them. Ask God to reveal your heart and to calm your mind in advance so that you will respond to people and situations in a godly way.

Along with prayer, how do we identify and then deal rightly with these triggers? Consider the following three steps:[6]

Step 1: Identify the trigger and the unhealthy thought patterns that typically follow.

Step 2: Repent of your wrong thinking by remembering the following three truths about God:

- *God is good:* "As for you, O Lord, you will not restrain your mercy from me; your steadfast love and your faithfulness will ever preserve me!"
- *God is present:* "As for me, I am poor and needy, but the Lord takes thought for me. You are my help and my deliverer; do not delay, O my God!"

- *God is working:* "He inclined to me and heard my cry. He drew me up from the pit of destruction...He put a new song in my mouth."

Step 3: Prepare your mind with specific, God-honoring thoughts you will embrace the next time a trigger comes.

Engage in gratitude for God's presence and goodness:

- Thank God for this opportunity to worship Him and to be changed.

- Thank Him for the reminder that we all need a Savior and God has provided one.

- Thank God for the reminder of past sin or hurt because it humbles us and pushes us to know Christ better.

Embrace a promise from God and His Word:

-   God will give me all the grace and strength I need to obey Him.

-   God hears my cries; He is working, and He is good.[7]

In dealing with various triggers that will inevitably pop up in our lives and ministries, may we be ever mindful of what is going on in our hearts and minds. May we continuously turn to the Lord in dependent prayer: "Lord, help me to show great patience, love, and humility in this situation by your power. Help me to do the things that I need to do to lead with godly patience. Help me to keep in step with your Spirit."

#8. Leading with patience helps us manage our "gut instincts" which can often mislead us in ministry.

One of the fruits of leading with impatience is that we make decisions more by "gut instinct" than we do through thoughtful, biblical discernment and prayer. While sometimes our gut instinct is right, many times it is wrong.

Here's the issue: In leading a hurting, declining congregation, you can't afford to unwisely trust your gut instinct and make poor decisions that create unneeded problems, harm, and hurt to people in your congregation. One of the key areas in which this is true is putting individuals into leadership positions too quickly. Many leaders rely far too heavily on their gut instinct when it comes to appointing leaders in the church. While sometimes we make the right choice, sometimes we don't. As a result, moving too quickly in placing folks into leadership slots they are not qualified or equipped for is potentially cause for a huge mess, both for them and for the congregation. Practicing patience will help assure that these disasters are avoided, or at least minimized.

Before putting anyone into a leadership position in your church, be sure to take the time needed to watch the person's life for a while. Watch them closely. Watch how they interact with people. Are they kind, warm, and gentle? What about following through on their commitments? Are they faithful, or are they flaky? Do they talk a big game but fail to follow through? Do they have a humble, servant-minded heart? Identifying these types of character traits in an individual takes time, which takes patience.

All of this is particularly true when it comes to raising up pastors (i.e. elders) and deacons in the church. You must take your time when raising up these leaders. A great deal of time. Don't rush this in any way; if you do, you will pay for it later. The Scriptures are clear about the qualifications for these two offices in the Pastoral Epistles.

Paul writes concerning pastors (i.e. elders) in 1 Timothy 3:3-13,

> The saying is trustworthy: If anyone aspires to the office of overseer, he desires a noble task. Therefore an overseer must be above reproach, the husband of one wife, sober-minded, self-controlled, respectable, hospitable, able to teach, not a drunkard, not violent but gentle, not quarrelsome, not a lover of money. He must manage his own household well, with all dignity keeping his children submissive, for if someone does not know how to manage his own household, how will he care for God's church? He must not be a recent convert, or he may become puffed up with conceit and fall into the condemnation of the devil. Moreover, he must be well thought of by outsiders, so that he may not fall into disgrace, into a snare of the devil.

He goes on to address the qualifications for a deacon:

Deacons likewise must be dignified, not double-tongued, not addicted to much wine, not greedy for dishonest gain. They must hold the mystery of the faith with a clear conscience. And let them also be tested first; then let them serve as deacons if they prove themselves blameless. Their wives likewise must be dignified, not slanderers, but sober-minded, faithful in all things. Let deacons each be the husband of one wife, managing their children and their own households well. For those who serve well as deacons gain a good standing for themselves and also great confidence in the faith that is in Christ Jesus.

Again, identifying these characteristics in a potential pastor or deacon takes time. It takes discernment. It takes wisdom from above. It takes prayerful patience.

#9: Leading with patience helps us keep the long-haul vision in mind.

Church revitalization is a marathon, not a sprint.

If you want to sprint in ministry, revitalization is not for you. Healthy, biblical revitalization simply doesn't happen overnight. It takes years of watching God bring a dying congregation back to life. For deeply discouraged people, it takes years of watching God transform them with sparks of hope that eventually ignite into an unquenchable fire for Him.

Leading with patience helps us to keep this long-haul vision in mind. Growing in patience helps us to relax and enjoy ministry! It encourages us to trust the Lord in the process. It empowers us to say, "You know what? The revitalization of this congregation is not going to happen in a week or a month or even a year, and that is okay." This is God's church. These are His people. Seeing this congregation grow is ultimately His work, done by His Spirit. We can rest in this reality even as we strive to love, lead, and shepherd well, with all that we are.

3 STRATEGIES TO CULTIVATE PATIENCE

I want to close by offering three specific strategies that I come back to often—three strategies that I believe can help each of us cultivate patience in our hearts and in our leadership. By way of reminder, patience is a fruit of the Spirit and, as such, will not happen by our own will. It happens as we humble ourselves before God, and He, through His Holy Spirit, grows the fruit of patience within us. But we have a role to play in this:

#1. Constantly remember how patient God is with you.

One of the ways we daily grow in patience is by recognizing that God has been incredibly patient with us. We should be continually mindful and thankful for this wonderful truth:

> "But you, O Lord, are a God merciful and gracious, slow to anger, and abounding in steadfast love and faithfulness." - Psalm 86:15

The Lord is faithful to His promises. He is faithful in His love. He is faithful in His grace through Christ toward us. He is patient with us. Unless we constantly remind ourselves of the incredible patience that God has shown us and continues to show us day in and day out through the Gospel, and unless we are constantly amazed by it, we will not grow as leaders who display Christ-like patience toward those we lead. We want to be pastors marked by the kind of patience that is seen so clearly in the person and ministry of Christ Himself.

#2. Repent of impatience, and plead with the Holy Spirit to change your heart.

There will be times in revitalization when, in our flesh, we will become impatient. Perhaps extraordinarily, ashamedly impatient. Whether it is with roadblocks to a change we want to make or in relating to a church member who is driving us crazy, we need to regularly practice humble repentance before the Lord for the sake of our own hearts (and, of course, for His name's sake). We require humble repentance that says,

> Oh God, change my heart! Forgive me of my impatience. Help me to trust You in this situation. Help me to love this person who is very difficult to love. Help me to display patience in the same way, Jesus, You have displayed patience toward me. I repent of the ways I have been antsy and untrusting of You, the One who is perfectly deserving of all my trust. Forgive me of the ways I have made this about myself and my agenda. Lord, give me a humble, loving, patient heart toward the sheep You have called me to care for and lead.

Of course, this kind of repentance and pleading with the Lord is not a one-time thing. It is an ongoing, daily practice that is critical to the health of our hearts and to the health of our God-given ministries.

#3. Trust in God's sovereign power and perfect wisdom in and over all situations.

One of the ways we can ultimately rest in the Lord and trust what He's doing in our congregations is to understand, believe, and trust in God's good, sovereign control over *all* things. This includes our churches. Stephen Charnock writes,

> In regard to God, patience is a submission to his sovereignty...to endure a trial, simply because we cannot avoid or resist it, is not

Christian patience. But to humbly submit because it is the will of God to inflict the trial, to be silent because the sovereignty of God orders it—is true godly patience.[8]

My life. My family. This church. Those who are difficult to lead. Those who hurt me. God is at work in and over all of these things. If we believe that God truly is sovereign, we can find rest and strength to be patient. We don't have to rush things. Again, remember, this isn't about your bringing about change in a church. This is God bringing about change in His perfect timing.

And so, we must continually grow in our trust of God's sovereignty, His power, His control, and His perfect wisdom in and over all situations. He is the all-wise God. I hope you believe that in both thought and practice. He is far wiser than you and me, and, therefore, we can trust Him.

Jesus Himself cried out before His death on the cross, *"Father...not my will, but yours, be done"* (Luke 22:42). May we echo these words in our own lives and leadership on a daily basis, joyfully pleading with the Lord to do all the things that He wants to do in our church, in His timing and for His glory.

FOR FURTHER REFLECTION

JOURNAL/DISCUSSION

1. Reflect on some of the ways the Lord has been patient with you in your life. How have others been patient with you over the course of your life?

2. Is patience something you struggle with? What would those closest to you say?

3. What are some of the areas in which you most struggle to display patience? With whom do you tend to have the smallest amount of patience? Why do you think this is?

4. What does the Gospel have to do with patience? How is the Gospel growing you and transforming you into a man that is patient?

5. Take a minute to reflect on the two components of patience discussed in this chapter – wisdom and timing. Journal about what it would look like if one of those components was missing and the effects that would have on your ministry.

6. A failure to lead with tactical patience (wisdom and timing) is one of the biggest reasons why many revitalizers struggle in ministry. Make a list of some of the unique and specific scenarios you may come up against in church revitalization that will take tactical patience on your part.

PRAY

- Ask for the Holy Spirit to produce patience in you that goes beyond your human abilities. Tell the Lord your struggles with patience and ask Him to change your heart and give you wisdom to know the ways to lead and the timing in which to do that.

-   Pray that the Lord would give you (and other leaders) eyes for the eternal perspective so that it provides wisdom and discernment and patience for hard times when it is difficult to be patient. Lift up those situations and people specifically who are difficult for you to be patient with and keep praying about those.

> *I therefore, a prisoner for the Lord, urge you to walk in a manner worthy of the calling to which you have been called, with all humility and gentleness, with patience, bearing with one another in love, eager to maintain the unity of the Spirit in the bond of peace.*
>
> *- Ephesians 4:1-3*

CHAPTER 3

LOVE

THE HEART OF GODLY LEADERSHIP

Love. There is nothing more important in the life of a Christian than love. In fact, if the two things that are spoken of us the most at our funerals are not our love for God and our love for people, then we will have missed the primary point of a godly life and ministry. Sure, there will be a lot of nice things that are said about us, but if people are simply sharing "what gifted leaders" we were or "what great preachers" we were, then we will have missed our fundamental calling. As pastors, specifically in a revitalization context, our fundamental calling is to love God and to love people with all that we are.

Mark 12:28-31 gets to the very heart of this truth with Jesus' response to a scribe who asked,

> "Which commandment is the most important of all?" Jesus answered, "The most important is, 'Hear, O Israel: The Lord our God, the Lord is one. And you shall love the Lord your God with all your heart and with all your soul and with all your mind

and with all your strength.' The second is this: 'You shall love your neighbor as yourself.' There is no other commandment greater than these."

When we feel like we are inept in so many areas as revitalizers, Jesus says that what is most important is to love God and to love people. I don't know about you, but this is such a wonderful truth to remember when I feel overwhelmed by all of the ways I fall short in ministry and leadership. We don't have to be rock stars at everything we do. But we do need to be pastors who love, by the grace and power of the Holy Spirit.

Reflecting on the love of Christ shown to us at the cross, John writes in 1 John 3:16, "By this we know love, that he laid down his life for us, and we ought to lay down our lives for the brothers."

Jesus loved us by laying down His life for His sheep. Our lives and leadership ought to increasingly be marked by that same kind of sacrificial love. Pastoral ministry in general—and church revitalization in particular—is all about people. This means we must learn to be Christ-like, sacrificial, loving leaders.

D.L. Moody was right when he said,

> "There's no use in trying to do church work without love. A doctor or a lawyer may do good work without love, but God's work cannot be done without love."[9]

Similarly, D.A. Carson has written,

> "No amount of good works, wisdom, discernment in matters of church discipline, patient endurance and hardship, hatred of sin, or disciplined doctrine, can ever make up for lovelessness."[10]

In 1 Corinthians 13:1-3 the Apostle Paul is clear on the absolute necessity of love when he explains,

If I speak in the tongues of men and of angels, but have not love, I am a noisy gong or a clanging cymbal. And if I have prophetic powers, and understand all mysteries and all knowledge, and if I have all faith, so as to remove mountains, but have not love, I am nothing. If I give away all I have, and if I deliver up my body to be burned, but have not love, I gain nothing.

If the ingredient of love is missing in our lives and in our leadership, according to the Apostle Paul, we are nothing. Nothing!

LOVE: THE DEFINING MARK OF OUR LEADERSHIP

The defining mark of our pastoral leadership as revitalizers must be love. Not charisma, talent, or skill... but love. Why is this? Consider five specific reasons.

#1. Love pleases and glorifies God.

Love is what God desires in His leaders. If our main purpose in life is to glorify God, then we bring glory to Him by obeying what He has commanded us to do. And what has He commanded us to do? Love God and love others.

We live in an upside-down world when we live for Christ. Whereas love according to the world selfishly focuses on ourselves and our perceived needs, love in the Kingdom of God focuses on God and others. This is the heart of Jesus.

#2. Love is biblical.

The Scriptures are clear: God is love, and He has made us to love. In fact, love is the most often repeated command in the Bible. We are instructed to love over fifty times in the New Testament alone. And this love we are called to show others—

especially fellow believers—flows out of the deep, deep love of Jesus for us. Christ Himself puts it this way in John 13:34, *"A new commandment I give to you, that you love one another: just as I have loved you, you also are to love one another."*

#3. It is who we are if we are in Christ.

If we have been saved and redeemed by Jesus, through the power of the Holy Spirit, we have been remade to love. We are now new creations in Christ, filled with the Holy Spirit of God that He might produce the fruit of love in us and through us to others. As Paul writes in Galatians 5:23, "But the fruit of the Spirit is **love**, joy, peace, patience, kindness, goodness, faithfulness, gentleness, self-control; against such things there is no law" *(emphasis mine)*.

Similarly, in 2 Corinthians 5:14-15, Paul says,

> For the love of Christ controls us, because we have concluded this: that one has died for all, therefore all have died; and he died for all, that those who live might no longer live for themselves but for him who for their sake died and was raised.

Joy comes in our lives and ministries as we love God and love people. The Lord has made us for this. It is when we refuse to love that we are failing to be who God has made us to be. For us to lead well for the glory of God, we will need to intentionally and joyfully live within our new identity in Christ, loving God and people with humility and kindness, hope and grace. Loving in this way is who we are now!

#4. Love is what our people need.

As I've said before, ministry is all about people. Leadership is all about people. Church revitalization is all about people. The one thing our people need the most is love. Biblical love. Loving leadership from pastors is what they long for because love changes people.

Jesus demonstrated love toward people constantly. The unlovable, He loved. The untouchable, He touched. He didn't see their social status based on the misconstrued laws of the rulers of the day, rather He saw everyone as sinners in need of saving.

Even though we've heard these Gospel truths so many times, such as in John 3:16-17, don't let the repetition lead to loss of significance and power in your life:

> For God so loved the world, that he gave his only Son, that whoever believes in him should not perish but have eternal life. For God did not send his Son into the world to condemn the world, but in order that the world might be saved through him.

Truly, God out of unfathomable love sent His Son to rescue and redeem a people for Himself, and Jesus faithfully loves His own to the very end. Shouldn't we then, as those called to shepherd Christ's sheep, see these individuals in our congregations the way that God sees them? Not as a problem, not as a burden, but as souls in need of being saved? Souls in need of grace and mercy? Shouldn't we love them like that?

In John 15:12-17, Jesus says,

> This is my commandment, that you love one another as I have loved you. Greater love has no one than this, that someone lay down his life for his friends. You are my friends if you do what I command you. No longer do I call you servants, for the servant

does not know what his master is doing; but I have called you friends, for all that I have heard from my Father I have made known to you. You did not choose me, but I chose you and appointed you that you should go and bear fruit and that your fruit should abide, so that whatever you ask the Father in my name, he may give it to you. These things I command you, so that you will love one another.

#5. Love is effective.

Pastor Mark Dance says,

> "Sheep will let you lead them if you first love and feed them. If you try to lead or feed them without loving them first, you may get bit, or worse, ignored...loving your sheep first is a much better pastoral plan."[11]

We don't display love for pragmatic reasons. However, the reality is that because God has called us to love Him and to love others, the most effective way to grow and revitalize a dying church is through loving leadership. If this is true, and I believe it is, then growing as passionate lovers of God and people should be the primary focus and goal of our lives. So, what does this look like exactly?

LOVE AND CHURCH REVITALIZATION

Let's consider some specific, practical ways we as revitalizers can lead our congregations with love. If some of these are currently areas of strength for you, praise God! At the same time, let me encourage you to keep growing in them. The same is true for those areas in which we are weak. May we humbly ask the Lord to keep growing us and maturing us in each of the following areas of loving leadership.

Pursuing Those You Lead with Words of Encouragement

Encouragement is love spoken. People come alive when they receive words of affirmation and encouragement. Often in the church and in our culture, we regularly hear words of discouragement. A loving leader combats this by building others up through intentional, consistent words of encouragement. As Paul encourages the believers to whom he is writing in 1 Thessalonians 5:11, "Therefore encourage one another and build one another up, just as you are doing."

Think for a moment about a time in which someone genuinely spoke an encouraging word to you. He or she saw that you were really good at something and wanted to encourage you to continue to do that good work. When that encouragement happened, it was like a joy bomb went off inside of you! Right? My guess is that this encouraging word caused you to care for and trust this individual more than you did before. My guess is that you truly felt loved by him or her. This is what genuine, loving encouragement does in someone.

As those serving struggling and dying churches, our leadership must be marked by life-giving, hope-filled encouragement! If you are not a natural encourager, the good news is that the Lord can change this in you. I can tell you from personal experience, encouragement is something all of us can grow in. We grow by watching and following the example of other encouraging leaders. We study what God's Word has to say about encouragement and then seek to live it out in joyful obedience. Ultimately, we begin to intentionally practice encouraging others. That's right; we practice. As with most anything else in life, the more we actually practice speaking encouraging words to others, the better at it we get. The more delight we experience in it. The more built up others feel by it. Over time, this practice of encouragement will become a habit of the heart and then, hopefully, a passion of your leadership.

Investing in the Growth of Those We Lead

We must intentionally invest in the growth of those we lead in the church. This is a key way to display loving leadership. Now, I'm not just talking about the congregation generally, in terms of feeding them the Word of God and helping them to grow spiritually. I have in mind here different leaders who are under your oversight. Loving leaders help other leaders grow and develop—identifying gifts in people, elevating them, and encouraging them in their areas of gifting. Scripture is clear that people have intrinsic value beyond their tangible contributions as workers, and as such, we must be deeply committed to the growth of each and every individual within our care. Find ways to equip them to become the leaders God has made them to be.

Unleashing People to Do Ministry

What does it mean to unleash people to do ministry? This might be a phrase with which you are unfamiliar. It simply means that we empower and encourage others to do the things God has called them to do. It means giving up control and asking the Holy Spirit to do whatever ministry He wants to do through our people for the sake of His Kingdom. Developing leaders in the church to do various tasks does not mean making people fit into a box that we create *for them*. Instead, unleashing people means intentionally creating ministry pathways *with them* in which they will thrive, and the church body and surrounding community will be blessed.

We want to get people "into the game" of ministry through using their God-given gifts. When men and women begin to use these gifts in ministry, they feel a sense of worth. They feel like they belong. They believe they are contributing to the Kingdom. They come alive! This is hugely important in a dying church. If we really want others to get excited about serving, we will spend intentional time getting to know each person in our flock individually, helping them identify the gifts, talents, and passions the Lord has instilled within them. This is when people move from the sidelines and get into the game! This is when congregations begin to ignite with new life and ministry focus.

Being Available to People

One thing you observe throughout the life and ministry of Jesus is the fact that He was available. And He was available to all different kinds of people. The rich and the poor. The old and the young. The educated and the uneducated. The popular and the outcast. He was available. He was available to give counsel to the woman at the well. He was available to spend time with Zacchaeus at his house. Matthew 19:13-14 records how Jesus was even available to love and encourage the little children:

> Then children were brought to him that he might lay his hands on them and pray. The disciples rebuked the people, but Jesus said, "Let the little children come to me and do not hinder them, for to such belongs the kingdom of heaven."

As leaders in the church, we can never give the impression to people that we are unavailable to them or that we don't have time to meet with them, care for them, or pray for them. Even if we are in a large church, we must create intentional pathways to be available to our people. This kind of availability is crucial to communicating our love for the flock. Of course, this doesn't mean that we do not have appropriate boundaries set up within our busy schedules. We must be wise with our time. However, what I'm saying is that we should always work to create windows of availability for the flock under our care. We must be deliberate with this; otherwise, it simply won't happen. As pastors, we are called to love our people. Part of loving them well is through intentional and purposeful availability.

Valuing Different Ideas

I don't know about you, but at different times in my life I have served under leaders who aren't very interested in listening to the ideas of others, let alone valuing those ideas. The best leaders—the most effective and loving leaders—don't operate this way. Loving leaders value everyone's contributions and regularly seek to draw out other people's ideas. Even when you as a leader don't agree with every idea that is offered, it is important to value different ideas and the sharing of them. Others know this, and they appreciate it. More than that, this valuing of different ideas brings about a sense of unity, trust, and joy on a team and in a church.

Let me offer a practical strategy for implementing this. One of the best ways to collaborate with others in the church and on your leadership team is to take time to regularly brainstorm together through "whiteboarding." It is so simple. In fact, there are hundreds of different brainstorming, dreaming, and evaluation whiteboarding exercises you could easily use right now! All you really need is a whiteboard, some dry erase markers, and a group of people ready to think, share, and brainstorm together. To get whiteboarding ideas, go online, ask leaders outside of your church, or just come up with your own with the help of other leaders in your congregation.

At our church, we love to whiteboard! In fact, we encourage all of our different ministry leaders to make whiteboarding a regular activity with their teams. Whiteboarding is a simple tool that allows groups, individuals, and leaders in our congregation to give feedback, to dream, to share ideas, and to feel like they have a voice. Whiteboarding also helps to create an environment in which we can discuss different ideas and opinions people might have in a format that is fun and encouraging. The goal of doing this isn't to implement every idea that people have. In fact, most ideas proposed and discussed don't go anywhere (and often during whiteboarding people can see more clearly why certain ideas won't work). But the win we are shooting for is helping people feel heard, valued, and part of the team. This is critical when you are leading others in the church. We seek to use these times together to help get leaders and volunteers unified and moving in the same direction.

In my experience, churches without whiteboards regularly being used for the purposes described above tend to be churches in which people have very little voice to share ideas and to dream. You can imagine where this leads over time. Frustration. People get frustrated when they don't have a voice, when they can't offer their thoughts on various matters.

Here is my encouragement in this area: As we seek to bring new hope and life to a struggling or dying church, we must help discouraged people share ideas and dream again! God, the

Creator of the world, is a creative God. He gave people the ability to be creative as well. Don't feel threatened by others' creativity. Encourage it, and draw it out of those in your congregation. This is what loving leaders do.

Cultivating Trust

Cultivating trust with people is absolutely crucial. I cannot emphasize enough to church revitalizers the importance of cultivating trust with people. To be blunt, the failure to win the hearts and to earn the trust of those in a dying congregation is consistently the #1 failure I observe on the part of those who struggle to lead a church back to health and vibrancy. If you can't cultivate trust with the congregation you are shepherding, they won't follow your leadership. And if they won't follow your leadership, this church will not experience turnaround. As hard as this is to hear, it is true. Cultivating trust is massively important as a revitalizer. The leadership you hope to exercise in a congregation hinges on it.

There is an equation I use often for pastors when talking about building trust with those in our churches. It is simply this:

Consistency + Time + Grace & Truth = A Culture of Trust

Let's consider each of these different components needed to cultivate trust as revitalizers.

#1. Consistency. Consistency in ministry means that we are predictably present. I've heard it said, *"95% of ministry is just* *showing up."* And that is really true. This reality should be encouraging on weeks when we don't feel great about anything we are doing in ministry. Simply being consistent is huge. Showing up. Being faithful, not flaky. Being predictably present.

Sadly, countless declining churches have not had the privilege of having a faithfully consistent pastor in a very long time, if ever. Many of these congregations have grown quite accustomed to inconsistency in their shepherds. You and I must change this. Consistent, predictable presence helps cultivate the kind of trust that is desperately needed when seeking to win the hearts of those in a hurting, declining church.

#2. Time. We like to think that our time is our own, but, in reality, it is God's. Our time has been gifted to us by the Lord to be used and stewarded according to His will and desires. This is a good thing. In church revitalization, it means a recognition that a great deal of our time is to be spent with people. Hanging out with people. Grabbing coffee with people. Having people over for dinner. Investing time in those under our care is critical for the cultivation of trust that is needed for growth to happen.

#3. Grace & Truth. Consistent grace and truth over time is critical to building trust and unity in any local church. On the one hand, we cannot build trust with people without speaking the truth. Sure, we can be consistent and sacrifice a lot of time, but if we never speak the truth, people will wonder if we love them enough to actually correct them and point them in the direction God wants them to go.

On the other hand, if we don't have grace, then our people won't want to be around us. They won't feel safe with us. We may be consistent, give them time, and speak truth, but if we are not gentle and gracious, we will be perceived as unapproachable. Both grace and truth must be present in our preaching, in our counseling, in our visitation, in our evangelism, and in every area of our leadership. Building a culture marked by genuine love and trust is vital to the health and growth of a struggling congregation. Remember…

> Consistency + Time + Grace & Truth = A Culture of Trust

Forgiving Those Who Hurt You

There is no way around it. As revitalization pastors, we are going to be wounded by those we love, by those in whom we have invested much time and energy. It is part of the territory of serving people—not a fun part, but a very real part nonetheless. For this reason, we must be prepared to forgive others, as difficult as it may be.

Over and over again, we must be prepared to forgive those who wound us. Jesus made this clear in Matthew 18:21-22 when Peter comes up to Him and asks, "Lord, how often will my brother sin against me, and I forgive him? As many as seven times?' Jesus said to him, 'I do not say to you seven times, but seventy-seven times.'" Loving leaders seek to forgive others in their congregation time and again, by the grace and power of God.

It is important to remember that many declining churches have within them hurting people. They are hurting for any number of reasons, but one thing is sure: Hurting people often hurt people. And, many times, pastors are the easiest targets when people feel the need to wound another. This is why we must be prepared both emotionally and spiritually for the hurtful words and actions that will be headed our way. More than that, we must be prepared to forgive.

There's a powerful picture we can reveal in absorbing both undeserved and deserved "shots" of complaint and criticism from congregants and in displaying a willingness to extend forgiveness to those who have sought to hurt us. We show the love of Jesus. Because the Son of God Himself has forgiven us far beyond anything we ourselves will ever have to forgive. May we take to heart, and put into practice, the words of Paul when he writes in Ephesians 4:32, "Be kind to one another, tenderhearted, forgiving one another, as God in Christ forgave you."

Demonstrating Gentleness

What comes to mind when you think of a gentle pastor? Gentleness is not only a biblical qualification for those serving as pastors in the local church (1 Tim. 3:3), but it is one of the most critical characteristics for effective pastoral leadership in a struggling church in need of change. Paul addresses the importance of pastoral gentleness when he writes,

> And the Lord's servant must not be quarrelsome but kind to everyone, able to teach, patiently enduring evil, correcting his opponents with gentleness. God may perhaps grant them

repentance leading to a knowledge of the truth (2 Timothy 2:24-25).

Look at that last sentence again: *"God may perhaps grant them repentance leading to a knowledge of the truth."* As mentioned earlier, we are going to have critics and opponents in church revitalization. The question is, how do we respond to them? While there will be times when it's appropriate to simply sit and say nothing, there will be other times when we must gently, yet firmly, confront people with the truth. There will be times when the most loving thing we can do is correct individuals by helping them to see their selfishness, their pride, their wrong in a situation. However, we must do this with gentleness and pray that the Lord would lead them to repentance.

Kevin Fitzgerald nails it when he writes,

> It is a big deal to God who takes care of his people. Imagine the immense price paid to purchase us, the price of divine blood. God doesn't want them roughed up, he doesn't want us to drive the sheep, to neglect them, or be bullying them. Remember when your children were little, you were very careful about who you got to babysit them. Think of the shepherd out in the field with the sheep and a rod in his hand. That rod is for the wolf or the bear. Never for the sheep. The shepherd leads the sheep out gently.[12]

How dare we as shepherds, as pastors, use the rod to beat up the sheep! We should only use the rod to protect the sheep as we fight off the wolves and the bears. We're called to shepherd God's sheep with gentleness.

Valuing God's Process of Growing People

In 1 Thessalonians 5:14 we read, "And we urge you, brothers, admonish the idle, encourage the fainthearted, help the weak, be patient with them all."

We are all in process. Every one of us. Theologically speaking, we know that the Holy Spirit is sanctifying us as believers, but our sanctification is a progressive process. In other words, our sanctification in holiness is growth that takes time. Thankfully, the Lord is patiently working in us, conforming us to the image of Christ for God's glory and for our joy in Him. It seems only appropriate then that if the Lord is patiently working in us, we must lovingly seek to be patient with other brothers and sisters, knowing that the Lord is at work in them as well. They are works in progress just as we are.

According to 1 Thessalonians 5, not only do we need to be patient with the idle, the fainthearted, and the weak, but we also need to be patient with the strong-willed, the arrogant, and the prideful. This can be a difficult task. As much as we would like to change people and change them quickly, this is not our job. Our job is to pray, to love, to speak truth with grace and gentleness, and to care for and shepherd the flock while trusting that the Lord is working in them just as He is in us. Patience is key in all of this. If you struggle with patience, cry out to the Lord and ask Him to grow you in this—to give you a heart of patience toward others that reflects the heart of Christ toward us. He has the power to make you a patient pastor.

Avoiding Rudeness

In our culture, we don't talk often about being rude anymore. In fact, being rude is often viewed in our culture as simply "good fun." It is comical; rude people make us laugh. However, Scripture has a different view of rudeness. In 1 Corinthians 13, we read that love is not rude. This means that loving leadership in the church is not marked by rudeness. Sadly, rudeness can easily bleed over into the leadership of many pastors in ways in which they are not even aware. Let's consider several ways rudeness can rear its ugly head in our leadership if we are not careful.

Four Kinds of Rudeness to Avoid:

#1. Inconsiderate Talk. Our words have power. What we say can oftentimes bring harm to people in lasting ways that we cannot even imagine. We can wound people very deeply with inconsiderate talk. Many times, we may not even realize that we have struck a nerve because of a person's history or personal convictions. This is another instance in which knowing our people well comes into play. However, inconsiderate talk also includes the more obvious like telling jokes that are inappropriate and talking about subjects that are not beneficial, helpful, or edifying for others. How easily do you fall into this?

May we take to heart Paul's exhortation to the Ephesians,

> Let no corrupting talk come out of your mouths, but only such as is good for building up, as fits the occasion, that it may give grace to those who hear. And do not grieve the Holy Spirit of God, by whom you were sealed for the day of redemption.
> - Ephesians 4:29-30

#2. Disregard for Other People's Time or Moral Conscience. Loving leaders are respectful of other people's time. If we tend to be people who are consistently late, we should ask God to help us become more punctual, even early, for the sake of others. It is understandable that we are all going to be late from time to time, but make sure you don't gain the reputation of being "the late guy," especially if you're a pastor. Simply put, it is rude. It isn't considerate of others. And the reality is that sharp, committed lay leaders in particular will not have a lot of patience for it over time.

Moreover, loving leaders sacrifice their own rights for the sake of meeting others' spiritual needs and moral conscience. Know that someone in your church will struggle with or be convicted of a certain area of sin in which you don't struggle or feel conviction. When this is the case, it is always rude, immature, and unloving to poke fun or to be insensitive to them in this. Honoring the moral conscience of others should be a top priority and practice of genuinely loving, Christ-like leaders.

#3. Taking Advantage of People. One thing you will see in virtually every declining church is a group of steady, humble, faithful volunteers and leaders who are always going to show up and serve. No matter what. Whenever there is a need in the church, these are the folks who show up every time. Here is the thing with this group of individuals: Over time, if we as pastors are not loving them, encouraging them, caring for them, and giving them breaks, they will burn out. Sadly, sometimes it is toward our best people that we show the least amount of intentional love. We take them for granted. We need to be mindful of this always. The last thing we want to slip into is unintentionally taking advantage of servants like these.

#4. Ignoring the Contributions of Others. We also cannot afford to ignore the contributions of others. We must regularly and consistently take the time to encourage people for all that they do. If we fail to do so, over time those in our congregation will feel unappreciated and grow discouraged. More than that, often they will eventually stop serving altogether. Paul understood this well. In fact, time and again in his letters we see him encouraging the saints to whom he was writing. For example, to the believers in Corinth he writes,

> I give thanks to my God always for you because of the grace of God that was given you in Christ Jesus, that in every way you were enriched in him in all speech and all knowledge—even as the testimony about Christ was confirmed among you—so that you are not lacking in any gift, as you wait for the revealing of our Lord Jesus Christ, who will sustain you to the end, guiltless in the day of our Lord Jesus Christ. God is faithful, by whom you were called into the fellowship of his Son, Jesus Christ our Lord (1 Corinthians 1:4-9).

Paul knew that he needed to build up the people in the church who were tired and needed rest yet were faithful to carry on the work of Christ. It is important to thank people and encourage others regularly for their hard work! We want to help our people experience the joy of the Lord and the joy of serving Him! Let us never ignore the wonderful, gracious contributions of others in Kingdom ministry.

All four of these areas of rudeness are evidences of a lack of love. There is no place for these in the local church and certainly not in the lives of those leading struggling, declining congregations. Let us ask the Lord to help us identify where we are falling short in these four areas, and then work to grow in each of them by the power of His Spirit and the Gospel that is graciously at work within us.

Insisting Not on Your Own Way

The wise pastor understands very well that the church he has been called to shepherd is not "his" church, it is the Lord's. Because of this, the wise pastor understands that he is there to lead this congregation not with a posture of power and intimidation over others, but instead with a posture of humility, service, and love. One implication of this is that the wise pastor will not insist on his own way. Demanding one's own way is not loving leadership. In fact, Jesus says that, for the Christian, our mindset should be the opposite. In Luke 6:31, Jesus teaches, "...as you wish that others would do to you, do so to them."

Instead of insisting on your own way, seek to be in tune with the needs of those whom you are serving, treating them as you yourself would want to be treated. Refusing to insist on your own way is at the heart of loving leadership. It's such a simple concept but is so radical and countercultural. It is a mark of leadership in the upside-down Kingdom of God! It is the kind of leadership that identifies a follower of Jesus who seeks to abide in Him and His Spirit daily.

Persevering Through Tough Seasons of Ministry

Loving God's people is not always a pleasant experience. It is not always easy. In fact, there will be really tough seasons in which we will want to give up and throw in the towel. We will be tempted to take a position at another church where maybe we won't have to deal with a lot of the tough stuff that comes with church revitalization. Or so we think. The truth is, "greener grass" is typically a mirage in both life and ministry. When we choose to leave for the greener pastures of what appears to be a healthier congregation, we quickly realize there are a whole new set of challenges to face.

Part of loving people well in a local church context is being committed for the long haul. It is saying to a congregation, "By God's grace, I am going to be with you through thick and thin. By the power of the Spirit, my desire is to persevere through both the good times and the tough times that lie ahead." This kind of pastoral perseverance is loving leadership in action. But it is tough work. In fact, while many pastors start off with the hope and desire of persevering over the long haul, the reality is that few actually do it.

Consider carefully the following, sobering statistics:[13]

- 1,500 pastors leave the ministry every month in America.

- Over 50% of pastors would leave the ministry if they could find another way to support their families.

- Over 50% of pastor's wives feel that their husbands' entering the ministry was the most destructive thing that ever happened to their families.

- 71% of pastors stated that they were burnt out, and they battled depression beyond fatigue on a weekly or daily basis.

- Only 1 out of 10 pastors will retire as a pastor.

Again, the reality is that pastoral ministry is hard. Church revitalization is hard. We have to count the cost. If we don't humbly and honestly consider the challenges we are stepping into, we are setting ourselves up not only for a huge disappointment but also a lot of pain.

I find it both helpful and hopeful to think of biblical leaders like Moses and David and how they persevered through tough seasons of ministry. While still sinners, by the grace of God these were two of the godliest men and leaders in the Scriptures. I am constantly amazed by how they invested their entire lives into people who often turned their backs on them. People who grumbled and criticized and rebelled against their leadership even though God Himself had called them and appointed them to these positions of oversight.

If this was the experience of men like Moses and David, we shouldn't be surprised if this is our experience too. But the good news is this: The Lord is with us through it all! And, if the Lord has called us to this position, He will empower us to do the work He has called us to do. What better way is there to display the love and faithfulness of Christ to a hurting, declining congregation than to persevere even through the darkest of times? When we persevere, we show that our ultimate hope and strength in life and ministry is Christ.

THE POWER OF LOVING LEADERSHIP

I've heard it said that the local church is to be a kind of display window for Christ's life-changing, other-worldly, supernatural love. As the love of Christ flows into the hearts and minds of His people and then out into the world, God is glorified, and the Kingdom advances. As Paul E. Billheimer writes,

> The local church, therefore, may be viewed as a spiritual workshop for the development of agape love. Thus the stresses and strains of a spiritual fellowship offer the ideal situation for the testing and maturing [of love]. . .The local congregation is one of the very best laboratories in which individual believers may

discover their real spiritual emptiness and begin to grow in agape love.[14]

I love this picture of the local church! It is a laboratory in which God's people grow in love with and for and toward one another. In order for our churches to become these types of laboratories of love, they must have the example of our loving leadership as revitalizers. May the Lord fill us with His love to overflowing, that it might spill out into the lives of the men and women, boys and girls, we have been graciously called to shepherd with the love of Christ!

FOR FURTHER REFLECTION

JOURNAL/DISCUSSION

1. What stands out to you the most in Jesus' love for people that we read about in the Bible?

2. Think about a non-family member that made you feel loved in your life – maybe it was a mentor or a teacher or a coach. What was it about them that made you feel loved?

3. What kinds of people are the hardest for you to love? Why? What kinds of people do you find it the easiest to love? Why?

4. Reflect back on a time when you were around a difficult person to love in the past. What are some practical ways that you can love people who are hard to love or may not be used to love?

5. In the world of ministry, pastors often get very busy and sometimes too focused on tasks – how can you make sure that loving people is a priority in your daily and weekly rhythm as a pastor?

6. Love is a fruit of the Spirit – take some time to reflect on love for people that grows out of the fruit of the Spirit vs. love for people that grows out of a pastor's natural gifting or strength.

7. What are 2-3 specific aspects of love spoken of in this chapter that you desire to grow in? What are some practical ways you can do this?

PRAY

-   Thank the Lord for His pursuing, patient, transforming love for you and the people He has loved you with in your life. Ask Him to grow the fruit of love in your own heart, by the power of His Spirit. Pray that He would give you love for people that are different than you or that are challenging.

-   Ask the Lord to cultivate an environment of love in your home, family, ministry so that He would be glorified in it.

> *"So, being affectionately desirous of you, we were ready to share with you not only the gospel of God but also our own selves, because you had become very dear to us."*
>
> *- 1 Thessalonians 2:8*

CHAPTER 4

FAITH

THE FUEL OF GODLY LEADERSHIP

"...the stress in these passages of sacred biography should be laid upon the words, 'by faith.' The mighty deeds of heroes and the obedient acts of pilgrim fathers are only told to us because they spring out of faith." - Charles Spurgeon[15]

When you stop and think about people you have known or read about who lived by radical faith in the Lord, who comes to your mind? What are some of the ways these individuals sought to walk by faith and not by sight day in and day out? In the same way, can you think of specific Christian leaders you have known or read about who led others by radical faith? What did this faith look like in their leadership over the years?

Leading with faith is a critical component in shepherding a church that is declining or dying. Hebrews 11, which is often called "the faith chapter," shows us some of the godliest people in the Scriptures, all of whom lived and led by radical faith in the Lord. Noah, Moses, Abraham, Jacob, David, Samuel, and the Prophets of the Old Testaments, among others, trusted God in a way that the world would have seen as absolutely foolish. These individuals had radical faith. They believed God, and God showed His faithfulness to them.

Today, we as revitalizers can learn a lot from these men and women. They not only show us what it means to LIVE by faith, but also what it means to LEAD with faith. Hebrews 11, verse 6, tells us that it is impossible to please God or to live the life that God has made us to live apart from a sold-out faith in Him:

> "And without faith it is impossible to please Him, for whoever would draw near to God must believe that He exists and that He rewards those who seek Him."

God is faithful to us, and He calls us to believe Him, to trust Him, and to live by faith in all that He is. This is true in our personal lives, but it is also true in our leadership as revitalizers.

WHAT IS BIBLICAL FAITH?

There are many different thoughts and ideas on what it actually means to have faith. But we aren't interested in just anyone's thoughts and ideas on this topic. We are interested in the truth. This is why we need to know God's thoughts and ideas on faith—what it is and what it isn't, according to the Bible.

When we go to the Scriptures, we see that biblical faith is trusting that God—with all of His attributes and all of His actions—is who He says He is, did what He said He did, and will do what He says He will do in accordance with His Word. We can understand biblical faith in the form of a simple equation:

Biblical Faith = Belief + Action

Biblical faith is not just belief. It is not simply acknowledging that God is who He says He is and will do what He says He will do. Biblical faith involves moving forward, acting on our beliefs with radical trust and dependence on our God who is faithful to keep His promises. It is trusting the Lord and moving forward with assurance and conviction. When we walk by faith in ministry, we bank on God's steadfast love and faithfulness in both our own lives and in the lives of our churches.

> "Now faith is the assurance of things hoped for, the conviction of things not seen." - Hebrews 11:1

In accordance with Hebrews 11:1, biblical faith leads us, as revitalizers, to move forward humbly yet confidently, believing that God is not done with dying churches! God is sovereign over all things past, present, and future, and He loves to display His strength in weakness. God loves to do the impossible, like breathing new life and vitality into a church most people have given up on. In faith, we move forward with assurance and conviction, trusting that God is in control. After all, this is His church, not ours. He loves His church far more than you or I ever could. He died for it.

CHURCH REVITALIZATION IS IMPOSSIBLE WITHOUT FAITH

While assuredly we need faith in every area of Christian ministry, it is absolutely imperative that pastors walk by faith and lead with faith in church revitalization. We, as revitalizers, are walking into church situations in which many will tell you, "You're crazy! There's no hope in this. Why would you give your life to that dying church? Why would you go there and waste all your time and energy with folks who may never want to change?"

Take heart. Put your faith in God. A.W. Tozer wisely explains,

> Remember that faith is not a noble quality found only in superior men. It is not a virtue attainable by a limited few. It is not the ability to persuade ourselves that black is white or that something we desire will come to pass if we only wish hard enough. Faith is simply the bringing of our minds into accord with the truth. It is adjusting our expectations to the promises of God in complete assurance that the God of the whole earth cannot lie. Man looks at a mountain and affirms, "That is a mountain." There is no particular virtue in the affirmation. It is simply accepting the fact that stands before him and bringing his belief into accord with the fact. The man does not create the mountain by believing, nor could he annihilate it by denying. And so with the truth of God. The believing man accepts a promise of God as a fact as solid as a mountain and vastly more enduring. His faith changes nothing except his own personal relation to the word of promise. God's Word is true whether we believe it or not. Human unbelief cannot alter the character of God.
>
> Faith is subjective, but it is sound only when it corresponds with objective reality. The man's faith in the mountain is valid only because the mountain is there; otherwise it would be mere imagination and would need to be sharply corrected to rescue the man from harmful delusion. So God is what He is in Himself.

He does not become what we believe. "I AM That I AM." We are on safe ground only when we know what kind of God He is and adjust our entire being to the holy concept.[16]

Here then is how we should respond: "Why would I go into a dying church and seek to lead it back to health and vitality? Because I believe in a God who is faithful and true. I believe in a God who redeems broken things for His glory. And I am going to bank my life and ministry on that very truth as it pertains to His church."

What drives us in revitalization? It's our faith. We believe that God can do what He says He will do. We know that He can bring dying churches back to life for His glory. More than that, we believe He wants to! He can breathe new life into the hearts of saints who are tired, weary, and downcast, while instilling within them a fresh, vibrant passion for Christ and the Gospel.

God is looking for faith-filled leaders. Leaders who have faith, not in their own ability, but in His ability to bring dying churches back to life.

LEADING WITH FAITH

It's one thing to understand what faith is; it's another to actually put that faith into practice as pastors and leaders. So, what exactly does it look like? What does it look like to lead with faith as a pastor of a declining church in need of new life?

#1. Faith looks like...leading people into a future that only God can accomplish.

What do we see with the great heroes of the faith like Abraham who trusted God with the life of his son Isaac? Or Moses who led the Israelites across the Red Sea on a journey in which they did not know where they were going? We see men and women willing to follow the Lord step by step as He leads them right where He wants them to go. We see leaders willing to trust Him with radical faith to the very places He wants them to be.

In revitalization, this is often what we find ourselves doing. We walk by faith, one step at a time, leading people into a future that is not always crystal clear. Often, we must lead people in a direction that we ourselves have never been before. It can be scary. It can feel uncertain. And yet, we walk by faith, trusting in the God who holds the future in His hands.

#2. Faith looks like...following God's vision, not people's opinions.

As revitalizers, it is tempting to allow the voices of others to influence us, whether those voices be from inside or outside the congregation. This is not necessarily a bad thing, but it can be. It all hinges on what voices you are listening to and whether or not those voices align with the voice of God.

Many pastors in our day, either knowingly or unknowingly, tend to give more weight to people's opinions than they do to God's. This shouldn't be. When we look at Scripture, it doesn't take long to see how the godliest men and women cared about hearing and obeying the voice of God above all others. They wanted God's will. They wanted God's vision. They wanted God's direction. Are we seeking after the same things? This happens as we stay on our faces, on our knees, in humility, begging the Lord daily to lead us where He wants to take us. We must say to Him from the heart, "Oh God, help us take the next step by faith. We want to do your will. We want to follow your vision. We want to follow Your desires. We want to be in line with Your purposes for our church."

#3. Faith looks like...dreaming and leading in a way that is "dangerous."

Too often in the church, pastors play it far too safe. We can get comfortable and stop living by faith. My guess is that it hasn't always been this way for most of us in ministry. There was a time when we had big faith and big dreams of doing incredible things for God and His glory. There was a time when we were willing to do whatever God called us to do. To go wherever He called us to go no matter how crazy it seemed to those around us. Sadly, many of us have long forgotten what ministering from that place of radical faith is like.

We need to be honest about this. If we have stopped leading and pastoring in such a way that we have to live by faith—that we actually have to have real, living faith in the Lord—then we are in a bad spot. It shouldn't be strange for us, even today, to step out in faith like those godly saints listed in Hebrews 11. But that is exactly what it feels like to so many pastors and leaders in Christ's church today. Living by that kind of faith seems strange. Dangerous. Unwise. Foolish.

Call it what you want, all I know is that Scripture is clear: Our great, sovereign, trustworthy God calls us to walk by faith and not by sight. Faith is the distinguishing mark of a truly Christian leader. Trusting the Lord with a faith that looks absolutely foreign and strange to the world—and at times even the church—around us. Dangerous? Perhaps. But when has God ever called anyone to comfort and safety? In revitalization, we need to dream and lead in a way that is faithfully "dangerous." Of course, this kind of faith is not the leap-with-your-eyes-closed faith that we see in the movies. This is a careful, prayerful step of faith that moves in accordance with God's Word and will.

There are countless stories of individuals throughout the history of the church who walked by radical faith—the kind of faith honed through circumstances of grave danger. They stepped out in faith and were rewarded with God's protection and a deeper relationship with Him. One such person was Corrie ten Boom. She stepped out in faith to save men, women, and children who would be victims of the Holocaust. Even though she was caught and ended up enduring the death camp of Auschwitz while losing her father and sister, she lived the rest of her life placing her absolute faith and trust in God. She said,

"...when we are powerless to do a thing, it is a great joy that we can come and step inside the ability of Jesus."[17]

This is living faith. Like Corrie ten Boom, may we as revitalizers live faith-filled lives, leaning daily on the "ability of Jesus" as we place our trust fully in Him.

#4. Faith looks like...continually trusting God with "the next thing."

Oftentimes, churches can become stagnant and plateaued after seasons in which they have experienced numerical growth, seen exciting new ministries begin, and watched many people come to faith in Christ. The main reason for this is because churches get comfortable. It is easy to begin to coast and stop walking by faith when everything seems to be going so well. This is true in our personal lives, as well as in our congregations.

I have met members of many declining churches who look back and say there was a time when their congregation truly walked by faith. There was a time when they trusted God to do crazy things that only He could do! But, over the years, that culture of radical faith was slowly replaced by a culture of comfortability and complacency. They stopped looking to God for "the next thing." They stopped looking for their next step of faith. That new initiative. That new outreach. They stopped dreaming about that next dangerous idea where if God didn't show up, it simply wasn't going to happen.

Over and over again, in both the Old and New Testaments, God says, "Remember. Remember who I Am, remember what I have brought you through, and remember what I did for you. Be encouraged! I can do that again and so much more!"

God sends a warning, though, to those who would continue to drift off into complacency. Speaking to the church at Ephesus in Revelation 2:1-5, the Lord says,

> I know your works, your toil and your patient endurance, and how you cannot bear with those who are evil, but have tested those who call themselves apostles and are not, and found them to be false. I know you are enduring patiently and bearing up for my name's sake, and you have not grown weary. But I have this against you, that you have abandoned the love you had at first. Remember therefore from where you have fallen; repent, and do the works you did at first. If not, I will come to you and remove your lampstand from its place, unless you repent.

Part of what Christ has in mind here is the primary love and faith that had marked their lives as new believers...but they had forgotten. Christ calls us to be men, women, and churches who love Him with childlike faith, no matter how old we are or how long we have been following Jesus.

The great author and missionary Elisabeth Elliot used to regularly say, *"Do the next thing."* It was a phrase that reminded her to keep her eyes focused on the Lord, trusting Him to guide her and direct her steps. It was a reminder to walk in faith and obedience one day at a time. This phrase came from the following anonymously-written poem that Elisabeth's mother had shared with her:

> From an old English parsonage down by the sea
> There came in the twilight a message to me;
> Its quaint Saxon legend, deeply engraven,
> Hath, it seems to me, teaching from Heaven.
> And on through the doors the quiet words ring
> Like a low inspiration: "DO THE NEXT THING."
>
> Many a questioning, many a fear,
> Many a doubt, hath its quieting here.
> Moment by moment, let down from Heaven,
> Time, opportunity, and guidance are given.
> Fear not tomorrows, child of the King,
> Thrust them with Jesus, do the next thing.
>
> Do it immediately, do it with prayer;
> Do it reliantly, casting all care;
> Do it with reverence, tracing His hand
> Who placed it before thee with earnest command.
> Stayed on Omnipotence, safe 'neath His wing,
> Leave all results, do the next thing.
>
> Looking for Jesus, ever serener,
> Working or suffering, be thy demeanor;
> In His dear presence, the rest of His calm,
> The light of His countenance be thy psalm,

Strong in His faithfulness, praise and sing.
Then, as He beckons thee, do the next thing.[18]

As revitalizers, we must remember to continually ask God where He wants us to go. What is "the next thing" He is leading us toward? We must regularly ask ourselves, our congregations, and our leaders, *"How will we trust God now?"* Or, *"How must we trust God next?"* We must lead our people patiently, lovingly, and kindly, yes, but we must encourage and exhort them to keep moving forward in faith as well. This is absolutely critical if we wish to avoid becoming stagnant and ineffective as leaders and congregations.

#5. Faith looks like...persevering even when we don't totally understand what He's doing.

There are going to be times when we find ourselves at a difficult or confusing impasse in our churches and ask, *"God, what are You up to? I know You are sovereign, but do You really know what You are doing here?"* It is in these challenging times that we must remember that true faith perseveres even when we don't understand what God is up to. We trust Him and His character even when we are confused by His activity or perceived inactivity.

This is where wisdom, discernment, and patient perseverance is so important in the life of faith and in the life of the faith-filled leader. Fear will so easily creep in when things seems uncertain or unpredictable. As shepherds of God's people, we cannot let fear override our faith. And yet, so often, leaders and churches succumb to this very thing.

Proverbs 3:5-6 reminds us, "Trust in the Lord with all your heart, and do not lean on your own understanding. In all your ways acknowledge him, and he will make straight your paths." Leading with faith means we trust God and persevere in faith, by His grace, even when we do not understand what He is doing.

#6. Faith looks like...displaying boldness and courage according to God's leading and promises.

When you think of boldness in leadership, what comes to mind? When you think of courage in leadership what comes to mind? If we are going to lead with faith, we need to be bold in our leadership. We also need to be courageous in our leadership. Bold courage forces us to depend on the Lord rather than ourselves.

Stepping out in faith as a church revitalizer can be frightening. If anyone tells you otherwise, they have most likely never led and shepherded a dying church. It can be frightening for all kinds of reasons. The problem is that this fear can cause us to take our eyes off the Lord and thus paralyze our faith. We begin looking inward to our own resources and begin trusting in ourselves in a way that we shouldn't. This is exactly what Satan wants us to do.

For this reason, it is critical that we battle against this tendency toward fear by the power of the Spirit. Cling to the same truth Paul speaks to Timothy when he writes, "For God gave us a spirit not of fear but of power and love and self-control" (2 Timothy 1:7). Timidity and fear are not a result of yielding to the Spirit; power and faith are.

While we find many examples of this kind of bold, courageous, faith-filled leadership throughout the Scriptures, one of the greatest examples we see is the Apostle Paul. It took great courage and boldness for Paul to start and lead new congregations in the face of persecution. It took courage and boldness to trust in the Lord as he helped Timothy and other young leaders grow in shepherding the flock God had put under their charge in the early church.

Speaking of the early church, these believers exhibited great courage and boldness time and time again, as they faced dangers of various kinds. When they were being hunted down and rounded up by those who despised them and their Christ, they held on with radical faith. Today, we must realize that the courage and boldness possessed by these early Christians is still available to us as believers. The Lord desires to grow these in each of us, particularly as revitalizers. He wants to give us courage and boldness to go to those places where revitalization is an insane risk and makes no sense to those around us. Why? Because the Lord is calling us to go. It is that simple. And God is calling us to go because He wants to use us as His chosen instruments to save His people. This includes His people located in communities and churches that many gave up on long ago.

God is not done with dying churches. The question is, will we take that first step and trust Him to give us the bold courage needed to lead with biblical faith?

#7. Faith looks like…leading through the possibility of failure.

A part of what makes faith, faith, is not knowing what exactly is going to happen. If we had everything all calculated out, it would no longer be faith that we are exercising. In church revitalization, we need to recognize that living by faith and leading with faith acknowledges the possibility of failure. It recognizes that there is risk involved. There is no guarantee that we will succeed, and yet, that is the very place where God wants us to be. He wants us to trust that He can part the waters and hold them back, that we might make it through the "Red Seas" that are sure to come our way as pastors and leaders.

While the ministry road ahead will at times look impossible, and we could easily throw in the towel and give up, these are often the times in which God asks us to trust Him the most and move forward anyway. To walk by faith and not by sight. As we walk by faith, we honor the Lord and trust He is going to do in us and through us exactly what He wants to do. This kind of faith pleases the Lord. Remember, as Hebrews 11:6 teaches us,

> And without faith it is impossible to please him, for whoever would draw near to God must believe that he exists and that he rewards those who seek him.

God is pleased with those who trust Him and walk by faith, even in the face of possible failure. Will you trust God enough to walk by faith, no matter what comes? The Lord is looking for leaders with faith like this.

#8. Faith looks like...remembering that leading in our own strength and power is not leading with faith in God.

Let me put it simply. If you and I create a church culture in which everything we do can be done whether or not God shows up, we have a problem. If the primary focus of our revitalization efforts rests on our personal creativity or our gifting in putting together slick programs and events—if we can do everything we are doing in our churches without God—then we are not leading with faith.

God is looking for leaders who lead in such a way that there are things taking place regularly in our churches that can only be explained by the presence of God showing up and moving in power. That's the only way we can explain it: God showed up! The only way we can make sense of a person who was so far from Jesus and is now growing in his or her love for God, is God Himself! The only way we can explain that this or that new ministry is producing much fruit is because God is moving, and He gets all the glory for it. Of course, we must remind our people that the Lord has given us skills, talents, and abilities to use for His purposes, and we want to be faithful with them. But we must be careful not to trust in these more than we trust in God. It is so easy to fall back on ourselves, on our own abilities, and fail to maintain a posture that says and believes, "Oh, God, if You do not show up, this will not happen. Help me to trust in You and not in myself. Empower me to walk by faith in You and You alone."

#9. Faith looks like...being willing to change directions as God leads.

There will be times in ministry when we believe that God is leading in one direction, and perhaps He is, but it may only be for a short period of time before He changes things up. Without notice, He may say, *"It's time to stop what you're doing and go in this new direction."* Or, *"I want you to begin this new program or ministry that you have never thought about before."* Are you willing to change directions as God leads? This is an aspect of leading by faith in revitalization. We must remain openhanded, completely willing to allow God to mess up our plans because He has something better in mind, even if we didn't see it coming.

Look, God is alive, and He is at work! It might be that, behind the scenes, God has been doing a work in your congregation or in your community that you as a leader are not even aware of, yet the time has come to implement the plan He has been preparing. Will you be ready and willing to go where He leads? Even though it interferes with your plans? Whatever it looks like, the point is this: Living by and leading with faith means we are open to move and change as God redirects us.

When we stop allowing the Lord to redirect our plans, our ministries become about us and our agenda, instead of about the Lord and His agenda. As revitalizers, we must ask God to give us radical faith that says, "God whatever You want, wherever You want us to go, we are willing to go! As crazy as it looks, as crazy as it seems, walking by faith in You is where we want to be."

WE MUST LEAD WITH FAITH

Churches that are declining or dying need pastors who lead from a place of radical faith. They need leaders who trust in the God who loves His sheep and loves the lost who have yet to come to Jesus. As we embark on this journey of church revitalization, may we ask the Lord to grow us in faith, so that we might lead from a place of crazy, humble, unflinching trust in Him as He guides us step by step.

FURTHER REFLECTION

JOURNAL/DISCUSSION

1. Take time to reflect on your life about a time that you walked by faith. How did you feel before you took that step of faith? What was it like to walk by faith before seeing any end results? How did you see God's faithfulness as you walked by faith?

2. Can you think of any examples in your own life of leaders who have led by faith? How did they lead this way? What prepared them to lead by faith? What was the effect on the people they were leading when they led by faith?

3. Think about the definition that faith is belief + action. How can you grow in your trust in God so that when it's time to move forward in faith you are ready to go? How can you cultivate this same trust in your congregation so that you can all walk forward in faith together?

4. Of the nine ways listed to lead with faith as a revitalizer, which of those come easier to you? In which of those will you have to really depend on God in order to live them out as you lead?

5. Sometimes our faith is dwindling and we need people to help us reflect on God's faithfulness and encourage us towards walking and leading by faith. Who in your life can you turn to that will encourage you to live and walk and lead by faith?

PRAY

- Thank God for His faithfulness in the past as you have walked by faith – be specific as you pray and remember. Ask the Lord to remind you of his eternal perspective so that it will fuel you to take that first step of faith in difficult situations. Ask the Lord to deepen your confidence in Him, His power, His sovereignty, His plans and His will so that your trust in Him increases and prepares you to lead by faith.

- Ask the Lord to give you impossible circumstances so that it is obvious to you and all around you that He is at work and it's not any person's doing. Pray that He would give you close friends who also are seeking to walk and lead by faith so that you can encourage each other.

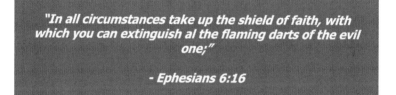

"In all circumstances take up the shield of faith, with which you can extinguish al the flaming darts of the evil one;"

- Ephesians 6:16

CHAPTER 5

PASSION

THE CONTAGION OF GODLY LEADERSHIP

"To pursue ministry but not having a passion for the gospel and fulfilling the Great Commission is like pursuing medicine, but not liking patients. I suppose you can manage along, but you will lack fruitfulness and joy. Most troubling of all, you will hinder God's divine plan for reaching the world for Christ."
- Jason K. Allen[19]

Can you remember your first experience doing ministry? Maybe it was leading a Bible study, or helping coordinate a mission trip, or perhaps it was serving as an intern or staff member in a local church. Whatever it was, my guess is that when you first jumped in and began to serve the Lord in this way, you were more than a bit excited about the opportunity. In fact, I would bet you were fired up! You were passionate about what the Lord was leading you to be part of, and everyone around you knew it.

Unfortunately, for many pastors and leaders in the church, the excitement and passion they first started with in ministry can begin to fade over time. While they once saw ministry as an incredible privilege and joy, it has become, over time, simply monotonous and routine. As a result, they find themselves drifting into a place they never thought they would be. A place of comfort, ease, and boredom. The scary thing, of course, is how gradual—and, at times, unnoticeable—it all has happened.

This is a sad reality for many pastors in the church today, and it is a huge problem. It is a big problem not only for these leaders personally, but for the congregations they serve. Passion that once burned hot has been replaced with apathy. Excitement has been replaced with cynicism. Joy has been replaced with melancholy. And the heart-wrenching truth is that this can happen to any one of us in ministry. None of us is immune to the potential of losing our passion and zeal.

Why is maintaining passion so important in ministry? And how do we grow this passion in our hearts and in our leadership? This is what we will consider in this chapter. I truly believe that leading with passion is an absolutely crucial component to biblical, effective leadership in church revitalization. This is certainly true in our early years in a declining congregation. Of course, this begs the question, what exactly is passion? What are we talking about here?

WHAT IS PASSION?

Years ago, I came across a quote from John Wesley that I often think about to this day. Wesley said, "Light yourself on fire with passion, and people will come for miles to watch you burn." I love this. It is true. People long to follow passionate leaders in the church, in the same way that heat-seeking missiles follow fire. The problem is that it can be difficult to find pastors and leaders who burn with fire—with passion—like this.

Of course, this is not only a problem for many pastors and leaders. Sadly, many churches are dying because they are filled with men and women who have lost their passion too. They have lost their passion for Christ, for the Word, for one another, and for the lost in their communities. Dying churches desperately need a fresh dose of passion that can only come from the power of the Holy Spirit burning in us and through us.

As for those of us called to revitalize a dying church, passion is a priceless aspect of our leadership. As Brandon Cox writes,

> Passion is something that can be faked, but only temporarily. We can only keep up the facade of passion for something for so long before people begin to realize we are not quite as invested as we have acted. Real passion burns inside us. It flares up somewhat uncontrollably and makes us do crazy things, like go to new places with the gospel, get personally involved in the lives of hurting sinners, and push others around us forward even at the cost of our own comfort.[20]

Passion is not an emotion that we can conjure up and sustain in our own strength for long periods of time. It is much deeper than that. Roger Willmore describes it this way:

> Passion is that fire that God ignites in our bones and in our souls. It is like the fire in a furnace that gives heat to the entire house; or the fire in a steam engine that produces the power that moves the train down the track. Passion is ardent affection; a fervent, driving, overmastering feeling of conviction with an intense sense of urgency.[21]

When we search the Bible, we see that passion is associated with other words such as zeal and earnestness. Each of these is produced in a Christian—including, of course, a Christian leader—by God Himself. However, while God is the ultimate source of our passion, it is our responsibility to grow in our passion and zeal as we yield to the Holy Spirit's work in our lives.

For example, Romans 12:11 says, "Do not be slothful in zeal, be fervent in spirit, serve the Lord." The Apostle Paul's encouragement in this verse is to dissuade believers from becoming lukewarm and simply going through the motions of serving the Lord in ministry. Paul is encouraging believers to pursue passionate, zealous ministry as we remain tightly connected to the Lord Himself, who is the source of our spiritual strength. In other words, our zeal in serving the Lord cannot be separated from keeping our spiritual fervor as we abide in Christ and His Word.

Another example can be found in 2 Timothy 2:10, where we again find Paul writing to Timothy. He explains,

> "Therefore, I endure everything for the sake of the elect, that they also may obtain the salvation that is in Christ Jesus with eternal glory."

Paul says, *"I endure everything..."* That is passion on full display! Paul understood that in order to reach the lost with the Gospel, he would have to suffer many things. The same is true for every one of us in ministry. With Paul, we must be ready to endure anything that comes our way. This kind of enduring faithfulness is passion in action.

True, Spirit-fueled passion is the only thing that would drive someone to be crazy enough to do whatever it takes to reach folks with the Gospel. Passion. Zeal. Fervor. Earnestness. This is what is needed. Indeed, Paul was a man on fire. On fire for God, for the truth, for the Gospel. In 2 Corinthians 12:10, he states,

> "For the sake of Christ, then, I am content with weaknesses, insults, hardships, persecutions, and calamities. For when I am weak, then I am strong."

And then in Colossians 1:28-29, Paul says

> "Him we proclaim, warning everyone and teaching everyone with all wisdom, that we may present everyone mature in Christ. For this I toil, struggling with all his energy that he powerfully works within me."

These are words that could only come from a man on fire. A man filled with passion that can only come from God Himself. He freely admits that this doesn't come from his own strength, just as it cannot come from ours. Paul was empowered by the Spirit of God, and yet, in leaning into and living out that power, he strives and he toils. That is passion and zeal in action.

One more example of passion from the life of Paul is found in 1 Corinthians 9:24–27, where he writes,

> Do you not know that in a race all the runners run, but only one gets the prize? Run in such a way as to get the prize. Everyone who competes in the games goes into strict training. They do it to get a crown that will not last, but we do it to get a crown that will last forever. Therefore, I do not run like someone running aimlessly; I do not fight like a boxer beating the air. No, I strike a blow to my body and make it my slave so that after I have preached to others, I myself will not be disqualified for the prize.

No laziness in this race! No apathy or lukewarmness. Paul exhorts us to run hard with passion. With earnestness. With long-haul commitment. Paul's entire ministry had threads of passion and zeal woven throughout. It is a reminder of the kind of passion that we need, especially in church revitalization. This is a difficult calling. It is one that we do not just go into lackadaisically. We go in with passion, believing expectantly that God is not done with this dying church. In fact, the best days may very well lie ahead.

THE NECESSITY OF PASSION

There are many different reasons why leading with passion is so vital for a revitalizer serving a declining church. While the following is not an exhaustive list, I do believe each of these are important factors to consider.

#1. Passion inspires hope.

A forest fire. Have you ever seen or experienced one? They are no joke. Think about the image of a forest fire with me for a few moments as we consider what passion looks like in our lives as pastors and leaders.

After a forest fire has decimated everything in its path and begins to die out, a single tired spark can remain and smolder within a tree. With the right conditions, a breeze can fan that ember back into a flame. In a dying church, folks will often remember the heyday of when their church was significant in their community and how over the years they have lost their flame of passion. The wind stopped blowing, and, slowly and subtly, the fire in their hearts and in their congregation was doused. The result is that this church is now running on fumes rather than flames.

As previously stated, in most revitalization contexts, those church members who have remained are very tired. They have little hope left for the future health or growth of their church.

For this reason, if we are not leaders who are passionate about the Gospel, about these people, about the lost, and about what God can do, we will not inspire hope, nor passion, in the congregation.

You see, passion is a lot like fire. And passion that's growing and spreading is vital in helping discouraged congregations see that God is still alive and moving! God uses passion to ignite fresh vision and fresh fire in those who are ready to throw in the towel. He uses passionate leadership to help hopeless congregations begin to believe that God is not done with their church.

#2. Passion ignites passion that ignites passion in a congregation.

Let's continue with the forest fire analogy for a bit longer. There are three ingredients needed to start a wood fire: fuel, oxygen, and an ignition source. If only two of these ingredients are present, there can be no fire. Now, imagine that there is a small grove of twenty cedar trees growing in a gully at the base of a mountain densely covered in a lodge pole pine forest. The east wind had blown all summer and had left the trees parched and brown. Even the cedar grove, whose roots were tapped into the deep damp mud, were bending from the heat. A dry storm rolled overhead, and lightning struck the center cedar tree. Embers glowed bright orange. The wind buffeted the forest. Flames grew and spread up the cedar tree's trunk and across its branches. The handful of trees that were growing close to the center tree began to heat up, and soon they too were burning. Their flames burned in unison, hotter and higher, as one united flame. The wind continued to blow, and the outer ring of burning trees ignited the trees around them until the cedar grove was completely engulfed in flames. Sparks flew on heated air currents, and the surrounding forest began to burn. As the flame grew hotter, the fire flashed over, and whole communities of trees ignited until the entire mountain was in flames. Can you picture this scene?

In the congregations that we are revitalizing, we will find tired, parched people who are bending from the drought of their dying church. They don't see any hope because time and time again they have watched young families and pastors come and go, often heading to greener pastures. Now we find ourselves standing in the middle of this church in need of much love, hope, and passion! When God ignites our passion as leaders, like fire we begin to burn. And here's what happens: The people who are close to us will begin to smolder, and soon they will start to burn in unison with us. As a result, their passion will, in turn, catch others on fire. This is how passion works. This is how passion spreads. Passion ignites passion, which in turn ignites passion. As those in a congregation begin to burn with passion together for God, the Gospel, one another, and the lost, their shared, unified passion will begin to flash over and start fanning out into their communities.

My point in sharing this analogy of a forest fire is simply this: Passion is contagious. Passion is like fire. Passion spreads. The truth is, passion is more caught than taught. This is true for any congregation, but it is especially true with a dying church where there is only an ember of hope left. When we are around passionate people, we catch their zeal.

Of course, the opposite is also true. When we are around apathetic, dispassionate people, our flame can be easily doused. The unfortunate reality is that for many struggling congregations, they have not been shepherded in quite a while by pastors who are truly passionate about God and the things of God. But God wants to change this. He wants to use *you* to change this!

At first, the tired and weary sheep in our congregations may look at us in our passion and zeal like we are a little crazy. This is to be expected. Don't be surprised or offended by it. But, over time, by the power of the Holy Spirit, our core leaders will start to catch our fire. Then other influencers in the church will catch it too. After a while, like an expanding fire, passion will slowly begin to spread to others in the congregation. This passion for God and for the things of God will then begin to overflow outside the walls of our church. The glorious result of this is that Jesus becomes non-ignorable as God's people begin to live out the Great Commission through word and deed in their surrounding community! This is what biblical, Spirit-empowered passion can do!

#3. Passion is a catalyst for reaching and mobilizing new people to become part of your church.

While I am no expert in the world of forestry and forest fires, I am fascinated by them. For example, one thing that amazes me is how the unified flame of a forest fire grows. As it gets bigger, it begins to funnel in oxygen and to form what scientists call a "fire whirl" or "firenado." Towering, swirling heat rises in the center of the fire column—sometimes hundreds of feet in the air—and the flames on the outside dip and wrap around objects, igniting them and drawing fuel into the vorticity.

Think about this. As we go, show, and tell the Gospel to those around us, the Holy Spirit does a similar work in and through us. He uses our Christ-infused passion to proclaim His love and truth to the lost in such a way that He opens up the eyes and ignites the hearts of the spiritually blind and broken, drawing them back to Himself. This is the power of God at work through His people!

As we reach out to those who are new in our community and to those in the surrounding areas, individuals and families will begin to check out our church. Maybe they show up to our worship gathering on a Sunday morning. Or perhaps they come to a new community group or Bible study we are starting up. Maybe they are open to having coffee with us so that we can share with them the vision of our church and the work of revitalization God is beginning to do. Whatever reason they decide to check us out, I can tell you one of the biggest factors for why they will come back: our Spirit-empowered passion.

People who see a pastor on fire with passion will often think, "I don't totally know if I'm on board with everything yet, but this guy really believes in this! He is committed to this! He is fired up about this, and I want to hear more." Of course, not everyone responds this way to passion, but, in my experience, many do. For leaders in revitalization, the vision that God gives us to see a church come back to life and vibrancy is so compelling, how can we not be passionate about it? I'm convinced that many people want to be part of this kind of ministry; they just don't know it yet. Let them know it. It's time to burn!

#4. Passion is essential for leading the congregation with vision and endurance over the long haul.

A forest fire is in it for the long haul. It doesn't die easily. It doesn't go down without a fight. Likewise, our passion is not simply something we must begin with in revitalization. It isn't something we must pursue and fight for throughout the first few months after coming to the church and then no more. No, passion is something we must continually cultivate in our hearts in order to sustain health and vitality in our personal lives and leadership over the long haul. We must fan the flames of our passion and zeal, that we might lead well with vision and endurance through both the mountaintops and valleys that are sure to come in the years ahead.

WHAT THINGS MUST A REVITALIZER BE PASSIONATE ABOUT?

We have looked at what passion is and why passion is important in church revitalization. Now let's consider some of the specific things a revitalizer must be passionate about. Clearly, we cannot be—nor should we be—passionate about everything. So, the question is, "What are the most important things for us to be passionate about as pastors and leaders in a church needing to make a comeback?" Let me offer seven that are critical.

#1. God and His Gospel

While it may seem obvious, the number one focus of our passion should be God. He is the reason why we do what we do. He is the One for whom we do it all. John Piper writes, "God made us who we are to show the world who He is."

Who is God? Sometimes, in the bustle of doing ministry, we forget who we are serving and why we are serving Him. He is the One who "in the beginning" hovered over the face of the deep. He is the One who said, *"Let there be light,"* and there was light. He is the One who separated the light from the darkness and made day and night before He set the sun and moon in the sky. This is the God who set into motion a plan of redemption for His people from before time began. This is the God who sent His Son to become a servant of all. Jesus, the Son who lived a perfect life, taught us how to truly live. He died on the cross to redeem us from our sentence of death and rose from the dead, conquering Satan, sin, and death once for all. He ascended to heaven where He intercedes for us, and He will one day return to take us to Himself forever. This is the God who chose us individually as His own, called us out of our sinful nature, and gave us Himself. This is the God whom we preach about every week. This is our great God and Savior! How can we not be passionate about Him?!

In Psalm 113 we read, *"Who is like the LORD our God?"* Who or what do we find more important than God Himself? Are we so busy doing ministry that we don't have time to worship the very One we are seeking to serve? Nothing and no one can ever compare to our mighty God who deserves our passionate pursuit above anything or anyone else! Our passion for God is what must fuel every other passion we have in ministry.

#2. Our Families

Our families are our number one ministry as leaders in the church. God comes first and then come our wives and children.

It is very simple: If we fail in our shepherding in the home, we are not in a place to be shepherding God's people in the church. In a very real sense, if our wives and our kids do not see that we are passionate about them—that we love them more than we do ministry—over time, this will be devastating to all. Sadly, many a pastor has lost his ministry because he lost his wife first. He lost his family. We have to put our priorities right. Our passion for God is always first. Our passion for our families is next.

There are few things more beautiful in the church than watching pastors and leaders openly and unapologetically adore and serve their wives and kids. People witness it when you hold your wife's hand in church, place your arm around her shoulder, or give her your undivided attention. They see you hug, encourage, and shepherd your children. This is important for your wife, important for your children, and important for those in your congregation to observe and to learn from. This example mimics God's deep love and care for us as His children. It is a testimony of how a man and leader in the church should honor his commitment to God's original plan for family.

Don Carson writes,

> "An elder does what an ordinary Christian should do extraordinarily well. He's a model for the whole flock. He's a picture of maturity for all."[22]

Sadly, your wife will at times take unfair criticism and critique from those in the congregation. Your job as her husband—and this is a serious one—is to protect your wife. It's inevitable: Whether ignorantly or maliciously, sheep bite, and they will go after your family. You need to stand up for them in a courageous, yet Christ-like manner.

I very much appreciate the transparency of Pastor Brian Croft when addressing the hard realities of seeing his wife suffer as a result of real pain that she experienced in the church. He writes,

> My children were too young to remember the chaos, pain, and hurt of the early years, but my wife remembers it all too well. And it had a tremendous effect on her. By God's grace, there is no bitterness in either of our hearts from those years, but I believe some of the physical struggles and depression my wife later experienced were in part a result of those hard years. It's one thing to be the pastor who is receiving attacks at his church by his church, but it's another thing to be the wife of that pastor. As a result, my wife suffered in significant ways that forever changed us both. It is the grace of God that neither of us battles bitterness, but years came off our life during those hard years we are convinced will never return… The pain of those early years will never leave my family, but in God's kind providence, it makes the fruit of what we see now in our church that much sweeter. Seeing a unity among the races and generations in our church, having a loving relationship with those who once despised me, and experiencing members loving each other and God's Word as it is preached means so much more because of where we started.[23]

What can we as pastors and leaders do to help our wives when this happens? First, we must be open and honest with them about some of these challenges that come in pastoral ministry. No pastor or pastor's wife is immune from them. Second, we must be prepared to listen to them patiently and lovingly when they have been hurt and are discouraged. Third, we must be ready and willing to extend to them much grace and compassion when they have been wounded.

In addition to our wives, we must be very intentional in how we love and lead our kids, not placing upon them unrealistic and unfair expectations. They need to be shown grace upon grace, just as we do. In ministry, our kids don't need their father to simply be their pastor and preacher. They need him to be their dad and greatest encourager.

We are called to be lovers and leaders, protectors of the flock of God. But may we never forget that our first flock to be loved, led, and protected is right in our own homes.

#3. The Bible

"For whatever was written in former days was written for our instruction, that through endurance and through the encouragement of the Scriptures we might have hope." - Romans 15:4

The Word of God is alive. It is living and active. It is inspired by God. It is the very breath of God. It is useful for teaching, for reproof, for rebuking, for correcting, and for training in righteousness. We must be passionate about the Bible. We must be committed to it first in our own lives and then in our preaching and our leadership. We need to lead from the Word of God and let it be the authority when we are trying to enact change in any and every area of revitalization.

This means we must beg the Lord, year in and year out, to increase our love for His Word. To plead with God to give us the same passion George Müller had for the Scriptures. Müller, along with devoting himself to prayer every morning, believed the most important thing he did each day was to give himself

...to the reading of the Word of God, and to meditation on it...that [his] heart might be comforted, encouraged, warned, reproved, instructed; and that thus, by means of the Word of God, while meditating on it, [his] heart might be brought into experiential communion with the Lord." [24]

#4. The Existing Congregation

We must be passionate about the existing congregation. I don't mean just "put up" with them. We must be passionate about them! We must love them deeply and sacrificially. They cannot be seen as some burden we are forced to deal with or as a means to an end; they are God's children to be cared for passionately.

Each individual the Lord has placed under our leadership is a precious soul we have been called to love, lead, and help mature in Christ. The Lord in His sovereignty and providence has hand-picked us to serve as their pastor. This is a humbling and weighty privilege, not one to be taken lightly. In fact, if we are desiring to revitalize a congregation but are looking past the very people who are already there, we are in the wrong ministry.

Again, this doesn't mean it will be easy. Most likely, it will involve a great deal of hurt. Writing about some of the painful trials he endured from the existing congregation the Lord called him to pastor, Andrew Davis writes,

> My biggest struggle through it all was to maintain a godly and loving attitude toward people who hated me. I was able by the grace of God to avoid public moments of anger, but I continue to struggle with unforgiveness in some ways, and God continues to work humility in me to shepherd people lovingly who vigorously oppose me.[25]

Church revitalization can be very painful, especially when you are attacked by the very ones you are seeking to serve and love. However, at the end of the day, we must remember that these are God's people. The easy ones and the hard ones. Those who exude great love and joy as well as those who don't. These are the sheep of His pasture. These are the ones we have been called to shepherd by God's grace and power, even when it might be the last thing we feel like doing.

#5. The Community in which the Church is Located

Joon Choi is right when he says,

> One of the most difficult challenges that any local pastor may face is the task of leading the church to engage their surrounding community. Although this is, essentially, a biblical mandate to a large degree, due to the fast-changing, postmodern culture, coupled by western individualistic philosophies, for local churches to engage the local community is becoming increasingly more daunting today.[26]

Revitalizers must be passionate about the community in which the church is located. We should ask ourselves, "Does my heart break for this community?" and, "Am I willing to do whatever it takes to get to know and reach this community with the Gospel?" Thom Rainer says that most churches in need of revitalization "really don't know the community in which they are located. If they happen to open their eyes to the community's demographics and needs, they are often shocked about their misperceptions." [27]

Pastors who are truly invested in and passionate about the communities surrounding their congregations will learn the history of the area. They will spend time getting to know the schools and the principals and teachers who work there. They will intentionally frequent the local coffee shops and restaurants, building relationships with those who work and hang out there. They will also network with other pastors in the area. These are the types of things effective revitalizers do. In turn, they fall in love with the community, recognizing that God has been working there for a very long time, and they simply get the privilege of entering into the story that He has been writing for years.

#6. The Lost in the Community

While most dying congregations are declining for many different reasons, most likely one of the primary reasons is that there is no longer a vision, passion, and strategy for reaching with the Gospel those who are far from Christ in their communities. Their hearts are no longer broken for the lost. They don't really think about them, and they don't regularly pray for them. More than this, in many dying congregations, the lost are often viewed as a danger or threat from whom they need to protect themselves.

Effective revitalizers, on the other hand, are passionate about reaching the lost in their communities—whoever they are, whatever they look like, and whatever their stories might be. They are willing to do whatever it takes to reach those far from God with the Good News of Jesus, longing to fulfill Christ's words in Matthew 28:18-20:

> All authority in heaven and on earth has been given to me. Go therefore and make disciples of all nations, baptizing them in the name of the Father and of the Son and of the Holy Spirit, teaching them to observe all that I have commanded you. And behold, I am with you always, to the end of the age.

#7. Raising Up Leaders to Share the Work of Ministry

Quoting Samuel Miller in his article, "9 Ways to Raise Up Leaders in Your Church," Mark Dever writes,

Wherever you reside, endeavor always to acquire and maintain an influence with young men. They are the hope of the church and of the state; and he who becomes instrumental in imbuing their minds with sentiments of wisdom, virtue, and piety is one of the greatest benefactors of his species. They are, therefore, worthy of your special and unwearied attention...In short, employ every Christian method of attaching them to your person and ministry, and of inducing them to take an early interest in the affairs of the church.[28]

Effective revitalizers are passionate, zealous leaders who are committed to raising up and equipping other leaders for ministry. We can't do this on our own. One of the most important things we can do to help not only ourselves but also our congregations is to grow and mature as leaders and developers of other people. We must work to multiply our ministry by asking God to unleash His Spirit in and through His people. Listen, developing leaders takes a lot of time. It takes a lot of energy. That is one reason why most pastors are not very intentional about doing it. This can't be the case with us. We have to be passionate about this. Declining churches—*all* churches—need more than one leader. They need a team of leaders. It is our responsibility to raise them up and mobilize them to serve.

Paul speaks of this very thing to Timothy: "and what you have heard from me in the presence of many witnesses entrust to faithful men, who will be able to teach others also" (2 Timothy 2:2). We are who we are and where we are because of individuals who invested in us. It is that simple. We have been blessed by others who took the time and energy to pour into us. What a gift this is! We must now do the same with others.

BE INTENTIONAL WITH FOUR TYPES OF PEOPLE

When we are talking about passion and our leadership, so often those whom we are around the most determine the level of passion we are able to maintain in our lives and ministry. More than any of us fully realize, we are deeply affected by the passion, or the lack thereof, of others around us. Dave Kraft, who has written extensively on church leadership, identifies four specific types of individuals who can either help or hinder our growth as passionate leaders.[29]

#1. People Who Fuel Our Passion

These are the types of people who give us life. They fire us up! Clearly, we need more time, not less, with these individuals. These are people who fuel our energy when we spend time with them. Now, obviously, these will be living people, but they may also be old dead guys whom God uses profoundly in our lives. For me, men like Charles Spurgeon, John Bunyan, and Charles Simeon fall into this latter category. These were godly, passionate men from whom we can learn through their books, sermons, and other writings. Kraft wisely says, *"What we are tomorrow will be a result of the people we meet and the books we read today."* That's true. We need to be mindful of the people who fuel our passion. And we need to spend more, not less, time with them.

#2. People Who Catch Our Passion

We need these people in our lives. They tend to be those in our churches who are very teachable and moldable. They are people we enjoy leading because they're hungry for God, and they want to learn and grow. They understand the vision of multiplication. These are folks that, even as we are pouring our lives into them, desire to take what they learn and share it with others. It is critically important to have these people in our lives and ministries. They give us life and provide much-needed encouragement.

#3. People Who Enjoy Our Passion

These are sweet folks! They're what I call "fans." Kraft describes them this way:

> Most people we probably know fall into this category. On the one hand they don't take a great deal, but then neither do they add a great deal. It would be easy to spend lots of time with these 'nice people.' They are fun and easy to be with. [30]

We see fans in the church all the time. They're folks who are quick to tell people how much they love our church, even though they only come every once in a while. They are for us. They are behind us. However, they will most likely never be "all in" with us. At least not to the point of major sacrifice. While they enjoy our passion, they are not individuals who give us more of it.

#4. People Who Drain Our Passion

There are a lot of reasons we can lose our passion in ministry. It may be due to a lack of intimacy with the Lord or perhaps hidden sin in our lives. However, a huge cause for the loss of passion is being around and influenced by people who drain passion out of us.

There are at least three types of "passion stealers" I have encountered time and again over the years in ministry. Be on the lookout for:

1. **The Complainer** – They always vocalize something they do not like or are unhappy about.

2. **The Critic** – Instead of seeing what is right, they always see what is wrong…and they let you know it.

3. **The Overly-Needy** – These individuals will take whatever they can from you…and then they will take and take and take some more.

We must be aware of these passion stealers and the effect they have on us physically, emotionally, and spiritually as leaders. If we give too much of ourselves to these individuals, our passion will drain and diminish.

In considering the four different types of individuals—those who fuel, catch, enjoy, and drain our passion as leaders—Dave Kraft wisely states,

> As a leader, I want to make sure that I am spending most of my time with those in categories one and two and to be careful and prayerful about allowing too much time with those in three and four. With His help, I want to be pro-active, not re-active. Those in three and four can and, more than likely will, take most of my time if I am not careful.

This is so true in ministry. Those who drain us will be the ones who consume our time and attention if we are not proactive in whom we invest. This is why we must be wise in finding and raising up leaders who catch our passion and, therefore, can fuel our passion. This is critical as we think about being passionate leaders over the long haul in church revitalization.

FURTHER REFLECTION

JOURNAL/DISCUSSION

1. How can you tell that someone is passionate about something?

2. What are you passionate about? How does this reflect your desire to see a church revitalized?

3. Brandon Cox writes, "Passion is something that can be faked, but only temporarily. We can only keep up the facade of passion for something for so long before people begin to realize we are not quite as invested as we have acted. Real passion burns inside us. It flares up somewhat uncontrollably and makes us do crazy things, like go to new places with the gospel, get personally involved in the lives of hurting sinners, and push others around us forward even at the cost of our own comfort."

4. What are 2-3 things that jump out at you when you read this as it pertains to the importance of your passion as a revitalizer?

5. Thinking through the four types of people who fuel, catch, enjoy or drain our passion, can you think of someone who fits each other these people in your life and ministry? How did they affect your passion specifically?

6. What is your strategy for making sure you always have "passion fuelers" in your life?

7. What is your strategy for developing those who catch your passion?

PRAY

- Thank God that He is a God who is zealous for His people and for His glory. Pray that the Lord would give you a growing passion and zeal for these as well. Ask Him to increase in you a passion for the lost and a passion to see not only your congregation but other struggling congregations come back to life for His glory. Ask the Lord to bring others around you who share the same passion for church revitalization.

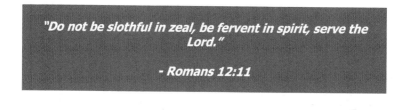

"Do not be slothful in zeal, be fervent in spirit, serve the Lord."

- Romans 12:11

CHAPTER 6

JOY

THE OVERFLOW OF GODLY LEADERSHIP

The "mountaintops" of ministry... How wonderful they are!
Mountaintops are those seasons in which pretty much
everything seems to be going great. New people are coming,
finances are steady, people are joyful and unified. Does it get
any better than this?! I have at times wished ministry was
marked exclusively by mountaintops. Of course, the reality is
that ministry isn't all mountaintops. We will experience dark
valleys, cold shoulders, and times of deep discouragement. In
fact, I have never met a pastor or leader who doesn't struggle
with the hurt and discouragement that comes with the territory
of church revitalization.

There are many things that can suck the joy out of us as
revitalizers. Thom Rainer has written about several of these "joy
stealers."[32] Consider a few of them:

Seeing the Underbelly of Christian Ministry

It doesn't take long after we have started serving in a new ministry position to realize that perhaps we have overidealized the situation. God reminds us quickly that we are working with, serving, and shepherding broken sinners just like us! We begin to realize that things are not as pretty and neat as we thought they might be. Reality hits.

At first, in the honeymoon stage, we walk into a church where the problems do not seem so bad. The warning signs are ignorable, and the issues and challenges are manageable. Eventually, though, our blinders fall off, and we start to see the ugly side of things. We start to see our people for who they really are—the good and the bad. The Lord opens our eyes to the underbelly of revitalization ministry. In these times, our joy can wane, and we can become discouraged.

Constant Criticisms

No one likes to be criticized. Criticism in ministry can suck the joy right out of you. It can be crushing. I've heard it said that constant criticism as a pastor feels like "death by a thousand cuts," especially when it comes from people we love and are sacrificially pouring our lives into. This is true. I know I've experienced this at different times in ministry. Criticism feels awful, yet it is a natural part of the revitalization terrain.

Fighting Among Those in the Congregation

Churches are broken because they are made up of broken, sinful people. Sadly, while churches should be filled with men and women who relentlessly encourage and build one another up, often the opposite is true. Bickering, gossip, slander, and infighting mark the history of many dying churches. Some of us will be called to go into congregations just like this. But there is hope!

As D. A. Carson writes,

> The church itself is not made up of natural "friends." It is made up of natural enemies. What binds us together is not common education, common race, common income levels, common politics, common nationality, common accents, common jobs, or anything of the sort. Christians come together, not because they form a natural collocation, but because they have been saved by Jesus Christ and owe him a common allegiance. In light of this common allegiance, in light of the fact that they have all been loved by Jesus himself, they commit themselves to doing what he says—and he commands them to love one another. In this light, they are a band of natural enemies who love one another for Jesus' sake.[33]

Carson is right. Our common allegiance is to Christ alone. We find our unity in Him. As shepherds, we must remind our people of this continually, leading with grace and truth, toughness and tenderness. In everything, we must point them to Christ.

Busyness that Turns into Prayerlessness

We will always lose our joy in the Lord and our joy in ministry when, because of busyness, we neglect our time with God. When our busyness begins to cause prayerlessness, we are in trouble. Big trouble. Here's what I know: The thing that will steal our joy the most in church revitalization is when we get so busy and distracted working "for God" that we fail to pursue intimacy "with God." Only as we seek the Lord through both prayer and the Word will we actually find the strength, passion, and joy needed to sustain us through the ups and downs of ministry.

Consider a few wise words pertaining to the absolute necessity of pursuing intimacy with the Lord in the face of ministry busyness. Charles Spurgeon writes,

> O that you were busy after the true riches, and could step aside awhile to enrich yourselves in solitude, and make your hearts vigorous by feeding upon the person and work of your ever blessed Lord! You miss a heaven below by a too eager pursuit of earth. You cannot know these joyful raptures if meditation be pushed into a corner.[34]

George Müller states,

> The point is this: I saw more clearly than ever that the first great and primary business to which I ought to attend every day was to have my soul happy in the Lord. The first thing to be concerned about was not how much I might serve the Lord, how I might glorify the Lord; but how I might get my soul into a happy state, and how my inner man might be nourished.[35]

Attacks on Our Families

This is an especially painful part of ministry. While we hear about unrealistic or unreasonable expectations placed upon "the pastor's wife" and "the preacher's kids," attacks directed toward our own are still trials that most of us pastors never anticipate. Friends, there will be times when our wives will take hits from other women in the church out of jealousy or envy. Sometimes our children will be criticized unfairly. These types of attacks on our families can create resentment in our hearts very quickly. We must be prepared for this. We must also be proactive in protecting our families and be willing to take the hits for them whenever we can, responding with grace and appropriate correction when necessary.

Sour Staff Relationships

Sadly, many churches do not have the best staff relationships. This is why we must work proactively to cultivate a loving and positive work environment in our congregation. In the beginning, we most likely will not have other staff, but, over time and God willing, we will build up a team of trusted, unified servant leaders. We must take care of our staff! We must love and encourage our staff intentionally and consistently. Joy is sucked out of us when staff relations go sour.

Inwardly-Focused Congregation

Being the shepherd of a church that is focused on itself, its own ministries, and its own activities, for the sake of the members alone, can be discouraging for a pastor who rightly desires to reach the lost. Those who see church as a country club which exists to meet their personal wants and needs can drive an outward-focused leader crazy, sucking joy right out of him.

Lack of Respect in the Community and Culture

I've heard church health specialist Thom Rainer talk about how, in 1990, sociologists ranked being a pastor as one of the most respected positions in our culture. Similar to doctors and lawyers, pastors held a highly respectable role in society. This has changed dramatically. Today, we will walk in circles in which we are disrespected or judged because we are "the weird pastor-guy," especially in some communities holding anti-

Christian mentalities. In our day, we can easily find ourselves in spiritual warzones in which pastors are constantly disrespected and looked down upon.

WHERE CAN JOY BE FOUND?

In light of the things mentioned above, how do we as pastors cultivate greater joy in our hearts? In particular, how can we foster joy in the face of the challenges that come with church revitalization? Throughout the duration of our ministries, we are going to have mountaintops with vistas of clarity and profound hope. At the same time, there will be seasons of trudging through deep valleys of discouragement where nothing seems to make sense.

Where do we go? Where do we as revitalizers find deep, supernatural joy that will help sustain us over the years? Where do we find the strength to "Count it all joy, my brothers, when you meet trials of various kinds, for you know that the testing of your faith produces steadfastness" (James 1:2-3)?

WHAT EXACTLY IS JOY?

Let's begin by first asking the question, "What exactly is joy?" Being a joyful person, biblically speaking, is not simply being someone who is happy all the time. It doesn't mean we don't have times when we are discouraged. Not at all. There will be times when we experience great discouragement. No, joy runs deeper than worldly happiness. It runs deeper than the circumstances of our ministries or our lives.

The primary catalyst for joy comes to us as a result of our salvation in Christ. Simply knowing that we are sinners who have been redeemed by the amazing grace of God should bring us a sense of great joy! But God does not stop there. At our conversion, He actually pours His Holy Spirit into us, sealing us, infusing us with a supernatural joy the world cannot comprehend.

Therefore, keep in mind the following:

- Joy comes with the settled assurance that God is in control of my life and His world.

- Joy exudes a quiet confidence that everything is ultimately going to be good because the Lord is on His throne.

- Joy is marked by the determined choice to praise God in every situation.

You see, true joy is rooted in a biblical understanding of the sovereignty of God. It comes when we understand that we have a God who reigns and rules over every square inch of existence. I'm not sure there is a stronger catalyst for joylessness than failing to believe in the sovereignty of God. This is particularly true in our ministry as revitalizers. However, what we know from the Scriptures is that the Lord is indeed sovereign. He is good. He is trustworthy. He is unshakable. He is all-wise. And because of these truths, we can find joy in Him in every circumstance.

Because, like patience, joy is one of the fruits of the Holy Spirit within us, it is the natural result of the work of God in a Christian's life, whether promised or fulfilled. In a sense, joy is the overflow of the Spirit's presence and work in our souls, which springs up and leads to passionate praise and joyful obedience to the Lord no matter what comes our way in life.

For this reason, joy can be found even in the "dark nights of the soul"—those seasons of deep darkness that we all as pastors encounter from time to time. As R.C. Sproul writes,

> We may think that the dark night of the soul is something completely incompatible with the fruit of the Spirit, not only that of faith but also that of joy. Once the Holy Spirit has flooded our hearts with a joy unspeakable, how can there be room in that chamber for such darkness? It is important for us to make a distinction between the spiritual fruit of joy and the cultural concept of happiness. A Christian can have joy in his heart while there is still spiritual depression in his head. The joy that we have sustains us through these dark nights and is not quenched by spiritual depression. The joy of the Christian is one that survives all downturns in life.[36]

When we look at these different characteristics of joy, we can see this is something we desperately need as leaders of struggling churches. We need a joy that is otherworldly. We need the joy of the Lord—and the peace and hope that embodies it—in the face of ministry challenges that are sure to come.

WHY SHOULD WE PURSUE JOY?

As church revitalizers, it's not enough to simply acknowledge that joy is important. Joy in the Lord must be one of the—if not *the*—greatest pursuits of our lives! Consider four reasons why:

#1. The Bible clearly commands joy.

It is interesting to observe throughout Scripture the many imperatives or commands that are given urging God's people to pursue their joy in the Lord. Just a few examples are:

- "You shall rejoice in all the good that the LORD your God has given to you..." - Deuteronomy 26:11a

- "Let the heavens be glad, and let the earth rejoice..." - Psalm 96:11a

- "Rejoice and be glad, for your reward is great in heaven..." - Matthew 5:12a

- "...rejoice that your names are written in heaven." - Luke 10:20b

- "Finally, brothers, rejoice." - 2 Corinthians 13:11a

- "Finally, my brothers, rejoice in the Lord." - Philippians 3:1a

- "Rejoice in the Lord always; again I will say, rejoice." - Philippians 4:4

- "Rejoice always." - 1 Thessalonians 5:16

We could go on and on with biblical examples. What we see throughout both the Old and New Testaments is that the Scriptures don't simply recommend joy; they command it! And the good news is that through both the ups and downs of ministry, God is committed to our joy in Him. As David Mathis writes,

> With our endless failures in view, it is such spectacularly good news that God himself is utterly committed to our everlasting joy in him. In fact, there is a sense in which he is as committed to our joy in him as he is to his ultimate purpose in the universe: that he be honored and glorified. Because our joy is tied to his glory. In the words of John Piper's poetic refrain, "God is most glorified in you when you are most satisfied in him.

God is righteous, and thus not indifferent to his glory. And the good news for those of us laying claim on the blood and righteousness of his Son is that he is not indifferent to our joy. Not the thin, frivolous, empty "joy" mere external circumstances in a fallen world can bring, but the thick, substantive, rich joy that can run deeper and wider than life's otherwise most joyless settings.[37]

#2. Our joy brings glory to God.

Some will protest and say that the pursuit of joy is self-centered and self-absorbed. And they are correct...*if* what they are speaking of is our pursuing joy and satisfaction in things that are not of God. However, that is not how the Bible speaks of joy. In fact, in Scripture, pursuing our joy and glorifying God are never to be in conflict. This is because we are commanded to pursue our joy *in* God Himself, and, as we do this, He is glorified in us and in our rejoicing!

To pursue your joy in God with your whole life is to honor the One in whom you are seeking joy. Of course, pursuing joy in God is very different than pursuing joy in the gifts of God. Most of us know how to enjoy God's good gifts. We know how to enjoy tasty food. We know how to enjoy the beautiful mountains. We know how to enjoy our precious children. We know how to enjoy the created things of this world.

The Bible, however, says that God is most glorified not when we pursue our joy in what He has given us, but when we pursue our joy in God Himself. God desires that we find joy, happiness, peace, and purpose in Him. In that pursuit, He is most glorified in us. Again, as John Piper has famously written, "God is most glorified in us when we are most satisfied in Him." Or, as we read in answer to question #1 of the *Westminster*

Shorter Catechism, "The chief end of man is to glorify God and enjoy Him forever." You and I were created to bring glory to God in and through our lives as we pursue our joy in Him!

#3. Joy is what sustains and strengthens our love for others.

Not only does the Bible clearly command us to pursue our joy in the Lord, and not only does our joy bring glory to God, but joy is a key ingredient that helps to sustain and strengthen our love for others in the church. Joy in the Lord is fuel in our pursuit and care of God's people.

In writing about the connection between Paul's joy and love as a pastor, John Piper writes,

> Every time Paul refers to his joy in his friends, he also refers to his joy in Christ as necessarily connected with it. His delight in other people is coming out of his delight in Christ, and it is aiming at their deeper and greater delight in Christ. [38]

Joy sustains and strengthens our love for others.

Remember, ministry is about people. And so, loving people well should never be a duty, but rather a delight! But if this truth is to become our day-to-day reality, then we must make our pursuit of joy in God our top priority. Our joyful growth in the Lord will overflow into a joyful love for those we serve. This is what true joy does! It overflows. Of course, the opposite is also true. If we fail to pursue our joy in the Lord, over time our joylessness will spill out onto those we have been called to shepherd.

If you want to lead a church marked by genuine love and joy in the Lord, it starts with you as a pastor leading the way in this pursuit. You cannot give to others what you do not have. This is why our constant prayer must be, "Lord, be my delight!

Be my joy! May Your joy that is in me fuel a genuine love for the people you have called me to serve! Even when life and ministry are tough, please fill me with Your joy, oh Lord!"

#4. Joy is evangelistic and missional.

Joy is supernatural. Joy is from God. Since joy is a fruit of the Spirit, true biblical joy is something the world knows nothing of apart from Christ. In fact, our joy will look strange to the world. Some will be annoyed by it. Some will despise it. Yet, because we as human beings were made for joy, there will be some who look at our joy and say, *"There is something going on there that I don't have, and I want it."*

There is nothing this world can offer that comes close to the joy of the Lord! In a world in which so many are discouraged and filled with fear and hopelessness, I believe the joy of the Lord is contagious. In a very real sense, it is evangelistic. Just like passion is contagious, joy is contagious as well. And there are many who are longing for this joy because they are longing for the God who made them and died to save them. You see, there are missional implications to our joy!

In your leadership as a revitalizer, it is your joy in the Lord that lost people will either shun or be drawn to. For those who are drawn, it isn't because they are drawn to you, it is because they are drawn to Jesus who lives in you and is drawing them to Himself! Joyful pastors stand out in a gloomy world. They stand out like light in the darkness, which is exactly what Jesus has called us to be:

> You are the light of the world. A city set on a hill cannot be hidden. Nor do people light a lamp and put it under a basket, but on a stand, and it gives light to all in the house. In the same way,

let your light shine before others, so that they may see your good works and give glory to your Father who is in heaven. - Matthew 5:14-16

Then the righteous will shine like the sun in the kingdom of their Father. - Matthew 13:43a

We are to be like the sun pushing back the darkness of this world with the light of Christ. We are to be like a city on a hill, calling those who are traveling through this life without Christ to come to Him. And our joy in the Lord is what fuels this light to shine more and more brightly for the glory of God. Dying and declining churches need pastors and leaders marked by this kind of joy.

The Fight for Joy

I'm convinced this pursuit of joy in the Lord is the greatest and most worthy pursuit of our lives. But know this: The pursuit of joy is also a fight. In a revitalization context in particular, we must be prepared to fight for our joy *every single day*. We are in a very real battle with very real challenges and temptations coming at us constantly. Each of these seek to steal our joy in the Lord on a daily basis. Let me encourage you to be mindful of two specific enemies against which you must guard yourself: **Enemy #1: Sin.** We must fight our sin daily by the power of God through the Gospel. Sin may satisfy your flesh for a moment. But, ultimately, it will steal your joy in God. We must guard against the acting up of our sinful natures. We must yield to the Spirit and strive to put sin to death by His strength. In this battle against sin, may we heed the wise counsel of Alistair Begg who offers three keys to dealing effectively with sin and temptation in our lives.[39] We must tackle it:

Immediately. The time to deal with temptation is in its beginning stage. Sinful desires and passions grow as rivers do. They are like rust; if left to itself, it eats away unceasingly.

Ruthlessly. We cannot play games with our sin. We must be ruthless with it. John Owen wisely said, "Be killing sin, or sin will be killing you." We must deal with sin and temptation ruthlessly. This is what Jesus had in mind when He taught that it is better to go to heaven with one eye than to go to hell with two eyes (Mark 9:47).

Consistently. Fighting sin and temptation is a daily battle. Because of this, we must intentionally and consistently kill it. This means we must daily pursue holiness by the grace of God. As those who are new creations in Christ, born again by the Spirit, our relationship with sin and temptation has changed. We are no longer slaves to it like we were before Christ. We can now battle against our sin immediately, ruthlessly, and consistently because of who we are in Jesus! Let us walk in the new identity and power that is ours in Him.

Enemy #2: Satan. We must never forget that we as Christians— and specifically as pastors—have a real enemy. Satan is a liar and deceiver who will come after us to discourage us in all sorts of ways. He will tell us that the promises of God are not true. He will try to convince us that certain people will never change. He will want you to believe there is no hope for your church and that God has abandoned you. Lies! These are all lies that can lead you to despair. But we must be on guard against them.

We must take Paul's words to the Ephesians seriously and put on the full armor of God ourselves in this daily battle:

> Finally, be strong in the Lord and in the strength of his might. Put on the whole armor of God, that you may be able to stand against the schemes of the devil. For we do not wrestle against flesh and blood, but against the rulers, against the authorities, against the cosmic powers over this present darkness, against the spiritual forces of evil in the heavenly places. Therefore take up the whole armor of God, that you may be able to withstand in the evil day, and having done all, to stand firm. Stand therefore, having fastened on the belt of truth, and having put on the breastplate of righteousness, and, as shoes for your feet, having put on the readiness given by the gospel of peace. In all circumstances take up the shield of faith, with which you can extinguish all the flaming darts of the evil one; and take the helmet of salvation, and the sword of the Spirit, which is the word of God, praying at all times in the Spirit, with all prayer and supplication. To that end, keep alert with all perseverance, making supplication for all the saints, and also for me, that words may be given to me in opening my mouth boldly to proclaim the mystery of the gospel, for which I am an ambassador in chains, that I may declare it boldly, as I ought to speak. - Ephesians 6:10-20

It is imperative that we keep the enemies of sin and Satan in mind as we shepherd and lead as revitalizers. They will be at work to steal our joy in the Lord and thus lead us to despair, hopelessness, and ineffectiveness in life and ministry. Ultimately, we fight against sin, temptation, and the lies of the Enemy through our intentional, daily pursuit of joy and satisfaction in Christ and the Gospel. Trip Lee, a hip-hop artist and pastor, put it so well in a leadership interview:

> I want to fight for joy because I don't want to lead from a perpetually dry place. Then it just becomes hypocritical, because we don't really believe what we are saying. Maybe we just believe it intellectually, but we don't believe it at a really deep heart level.

So, when we say to someone that Jesus satisfies your soul, we say that not from our own actual experience, but because we think it is what we are supposed to say. It can turn into hypocrisy very quickly. I think it can quickly turn into simply mimicking words.

At the heart of my ability to lead other people well is enjoying Jesus myself. Then I get to say, "Here is where I found that joy in the Scriptures, in Jesus. Come along with me on this journey," instead of saying, "Hey, I heard about this place way out there and I want to tell you about what I think it is like."[40]

We share what we love and believe in. If we know and pursue the joy of the Lord in our own lives, we will be equipped to share the joy of the Lord with those we lead and serve because we have experienced it ourselves. In ministry, we are not only fighting for our joy, we are fighting for others' joy as well.

KEEP FIGHTING!

Make no mistake, pursuing our joy in the Lord is one of the most important fights of our lives and our ministries.

Mark Altrogge writes,

God promises his children joy, and many times he fills us with it without our asking. But at other times, especially when we go through trials, we must fight for it. Much of the battle lies in fighting to believe God's Word.

For some the battle for joy is much harder than others. Some must deal with their own tendencies of being downcast. Depression and hard, long, sad afflictions can make Jesus' joy seem beyond reach. Yet God's Word says it's his intent to give us his joy both in this life and especially in the next.[41]

In light of this reality, how do we keep fighting for joy on a daily basis in ministry? Where do we find the strength to fight? Let me encourage you to spend some time thinking through and praying over the following strategies. Which of these strategies can you begin to apply even now?

TWENTY-FIVE STRATEGIES TO HELP YOU FIGHT FOR JOY IN CHRIST [42]

1. Praise God for the cross: for His mercy and grace in saving you.

2. Thank Him for all His spiritual benefits: forgiveness, adoption, the Word, spiritual gifts, the church.

3. Ask Jesus to fill you with His own joy (see John 15:11).

4. Thank Him for His steadfast love that never ceases.

5. Thank God for your temporal blessings: for your spouse or for the blessings of being single, kids, health, sight, food, strength, home, computer, and coffee.

6. Praise God for His attributes: His greatness, sovereignty, goodness, love, wisdom, and power.

7. Praise Jesus for being a compassionate high priest who intercedes for you.

8. Thank Him for all the specific good He is producing in you through trials: patience, perseverance, and faith.

9. Thank God for His past faithfulness.

10. Give to the kingdom.

11. Give to the poor.

12. Serve others (see Philippians 1:25).

13. Don't dwell on whether or not you are joyful. Try to forget yourself.

14. Thank the Lord that He is making you like Christ.

15. Seek God's presence in prayer (Psalm 16:11; Psalm 43:4).

16. Read the Word – it produces joy (Psalm 119:111).

17. Thank God that He will never turn away from doing good to you.

18. Ask others to pray for God to fill you with joy.

19. Ask the Holy Spirit to produce the fruit of joy in you.

20. Confess your sins to God and ask Him to restore the joy of your salvation (Psalm 51:12).

21. Memorize God's promises to give you joy and ask Him to fulfill them (John 16:24; Romans 14:17, 15:13; Psalm 4:7, 30:5, 68:3, 97:11, 126:6).

22. Consider others who have it much worse than you.

23. Pray for others who are suffering.

24. Contemplate the joys of heaven and the world to come.

25. Read John Piper's book, *When I Don't Desire God: How to Fight for Joy.*

Joy is something we desperately need in our leadership. Joy is something that declining and dying churches desperately need as well. Pastors and church leaders, may God through His Spirit use us to be the instruments and the catalysts to help bring about joy in our congregations once again. Let's fight for joy! For ourselves, for others, and for the glory of God.

FOR FURTHER REFLECTION

JOURNAL/DISCUSSION

1. What do you presently enjoy most about ministry to God's people? Make a list of these things that bring you joy!

2. In your personal life and ministry, what have been some "joy stealers" that you have consistently had to battle against?

3. What have been some effective ways that you have learned to fight for joy in these circumstances (From Question #2)?

4. What role does Christian community play in fighting for joy?

5. How does our understanding of who God is affect our ability to be joyful in ministry?

6. How might the challenges of church revitalization specifically present obstacles to our joy in the Lord?

7. What are some of the potential consequences of leading from a place that is not rooted in joy?

8. What are some "false idols" in ministry that you might be tempted to find joy and satisfaction in, rather than finding it in Christ?

PRAY

- Thank the Lord for His gift of salvation in Christ and the joy that comes from knowing Him! Ask God to increase your joy in Him, that He would daily show you that He is better and more satisfying than anything this world has to offer. Finally, ask the

Lord to help you lead with joy as you seek to love and shepherd God's people. The Lord loves you and is with you.

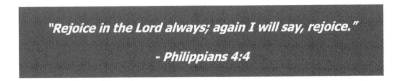

"Rejoice in the Lord always; again I will say, rejoice."

- Philippians 4:4

NOTES

[1] I have a written the book, *Who will Preach?: Raising Up Shepherd Preachers in Your Church* to help you begin to intentionally raise up preachers in your church. I truly believe that developing other preachers in your congregation will not only be valuable for those being developed, but it will be healthy for the lead preaching pastor, along with the entire congregation.

[2] Some of these suggestions have been adapted from C.J. Mahaney's excellent book, *Humility: True Greatness* (Colorado Springs, CO: Multnomah Publishers, 2005).

[3] Justin Taylor, "Easily Edified," *thegospelcoalition.org*, accessed November 12, 2018, https://www.thegospelcoalition.org/blogs/justin-taylor/easily-edified.

[4] Albert Mohler, "Patience is Not Optional for the Christian," *Ligonier.org*, accessed November 12, 2018. https://www.ligonier.org/blog/patience-not-optional-christian/.

[5] Sam Storms, "Why Patience Doesn't Come Naturally," *Samstorms.com*, accessed November 12, 2018, http://www.samstorms.com/enjoying-god-blog/post/why-patience-doesnt-come-naturally.

[6] Adapted from Andrea Lee's article, "Troubled by Triggers," *biblicalcounselingcoalition.org*, accessed November 12, 2018, https://biblicalcounselingcoalition.org/2018/03/20/troubled-by-triggers/.

[7] Ibid.

[8] William Plumber, "Vital Godliness: A Treatise on Experimental and Practical Piety," *gracegems.org*, accessed November 12, 2018, http://www.gracegems.org/24/vital_godliness22.htm.

[9] Alexander Strauch, *Leading with Love*, (Littleton, CO: Lewis & Roth Publishers, 2006), 8.

[10] D. A. Carson, "A Church That Does All the Right Things, But...," *Christianity Today* (June 29, 1979): 30.

[11] Mark Dance. "Two Things Pastors Must Do Before Leading," *Facts and Trends*, accessed November 12, 2018,

https://www.lifeway.com/pastors/2016/11/02/2-things-pastors-must-do-before-leading.

[12] Kevin Fitzgerald, "People Skills," *Biblicaleldership.com,* accessed November 12, 2018, https://biblicaleldership.com/effective-shepherding-172/leading-gods-flock-0/people-skills/people-skills-4.

[13] "Statistics on Pastors: 2016 update. Research on the Happenings in Pastors' Personal and Church Lives." *Into Thy Word,* www.churchleadership.org, accessed November 12, 2018. https://files.stablerack.com/webfiles/71795/pastorsstatWP2016.pdf.

[14] Paul E. Billheimer in Robert L. Peterson and Alexander Strauch, *Agape Leadership,* (Littleton, CO: Lewis & Roth Publishers, 1991), 9-10.

[15] C.H. Spurgeon, "The Hiding of Moses by Faith," *spugeongems.org,* accessed November 12, 2018, http://www.spurgeongems.org/vols22-24/chs1421.pdf.

[16] A.W. Tozer, *That Incredible Christian: How Heaven's Children Live on Earth,* (Camp Hill, Pennsylvania: Wing Spread Publishers, 1964) 22.

[17] Corrie Ten Boom, *Jesus is Victor,* (Tarrytown, New York: Revell Company, 1971), 110.

[18] Ray Van Nest "Do the Next thing," *rayvannestr.com,* accessed November 12, 2018, http://rayvanneste.com/?p=157.

[19] Jason K. Allen, "The One Passion Every Pastor Must Have," *ftc.org,* accessed November 12, 2018, https://ftc.co/resource-library/blog-entries/the-one-passion-every-pastor-must-have .

[20] Brandon Cox, "Passionate Leadership is Highly Biblical," *BrandonACox.com,* accessed November 12, 2018, http://brandonacox.com/leadership/passionate-leadership-is-highly-biblical.

[21] Roger D. Willmore, "Passion In Ministry," *SBClife.net,* accessed November 12, 2018, http://www.sbclife.net/article/1149/passion-in-ministry.

[22] Mark Dever, "9 Ways to Raise Up Leaders in Your Church," *thegospelcoalition.org,* accessed November 12, 2018, https://www.thegospelcoalition.org/article/9-ways-to-raise-up-leaders-in-your-church/.

[23] R. Albert Mohler Jr., *A Guide to Church Revitalization, Guide Book No. 005,* (Louisville, KY: SBTS Press, 2015) 77-78.

[24] George Muller, "George Muller on Personal Devotions," *georgemuller.org,* accessed November 12, 2018, https://www.georgemuller.org/uploads/4/8/6/5/48652749/george_muller_on_personal_devotions.pdf.

[25] Mohler, "A Guide to Church Revitalization," 83.

[26] Joon Choi, "Leading the Church to Engage the Community," *NAMB,* Replant Blog, accessed November 12, 2018, https://www.namb.net/replant-blog/leading-the-church-to-engage-the-community.

[27] Thom S. Rainer, "Ten Roadblocks to Church Revitalization," *Thomrainer.com,* accessed November 12, 2018, https://thomrainer.com/2017/07/ten-roadblocks-church-revitalization/.

[28] Mark Dever, "9 Ways to Raise Up Leaders in Your Church," *thegospelcoalition.org,* accessed June 5, 2017, https://www.thegospelcoalition.org/article/9-ways-to-raise-up-leaders-in-your-church.

[29] Dave Kraft, "Does Your Passion Have a Slow Leak?" *Davekraft.org,* accessed November 12, 2018, www.davekraft.org/posts/2014/1/19/does-your-passion-have-a-slow-leak.html.

[30] Ibid.

[31] Brandon Cox, "Passionate Leadership is Highly Biblical," *BrandonACox.com,* accessed November 12, 2018, http://brandonacox.com/leadership/passionate-leadership-is-highly-biblical.

[32] Thom S Rainer, "Ten Joy Stealers in Ministry (And How to Get It Back)," *Thomrainer.com,* accessed November 12, 2018, http://thomrainer.com/2015/02/ten-joy-stealers-ministry-get-back/.

[33] D.A. Carson, *Love in Hard Places,* (Wheaton, Illinois: Crossway Books, 2002), 61.

[34] C.H. Spurgeon, "Sermons of Rev. C. H. Spurgeon of London, Ninth Series" (New York: Robert Carter & Brothers, 1883), 329.

[35] George Muller, John Piper, "The Marks of a Spiritual Leader" desiringgod.org, accessed November 12, 2018, https://www.desiringgod.org/articles/the-marks-of-a-spiritual-leader.

[36] R.C. Sproul, "Spiritual Depression: The Dark Night of the Soul," *Ligonier.org,* accessed November 12, 2018, https://www.ligonier.org/blog/the-dark-night-of-the-soul.

[37] David Mathis, "Joy Is Not Optional, Why Your Happiness Matters To God," *desiringgod.org,* accessed November 12, 2018, https://www.desiringgod.org/articles/joy-is-not-optional.

[38] John Piper, "How Does Joy Overflow in Love?" *desiringgod.org,* accessed November 12, 2018, https://www.desiringgod.org/articles/how-does-joy-overflow-in-love.

[39] Alistair Begg, "Temptation – James 1:12-15," *Truthforlife.org,* accessed November 13, 2018, http://tflmedia.s3.amazonaws.com/free_downloads/2861-temptation.

[40] Trip Lee, "Leadership Requires the Pursuit of Joy," August 29, 2016, desiringgod.org, https://www.desiringgod.org/articles/leadership-requires-the-pursuit-of-joy.

[41] Mark Altrogge, "25 Ways to Pursue Joy in Christ," *theblazingcenter.com,* March 13, 2011, https://theblazingcenter.com/2011/03/25-ways-to-pursue-joy-in-christ.html.

[42] Ibid.

The **Starting Right in Church Revitalization** book series focuses on key areas of pastoral ministry crucial in turning around a declining church. The goal of this series is to help educate, equip, and encourage pastors and leaders called specifically to serve these congregations. Each book is aimed at helping individuals start well in their ministry, building a strong foundation that will help bring long term health, growth, and multiplication to dying churches in North America and to the ends of the earth.

STARTING RIGHT IN CHURCH REVITALIZATION

Get the resource which is empowering
a movement of church revitalization.

"Mark Hallock is one of the most important voices in this unprecedented
need in the modern day to revitalize dying churches. *Replant Roadmap* is
sure to become the practical how-to guide to lead this next generation
into this noble work."

Brian Croft, Senior Pastor, Auburndale Baptist Church; Senior Fellow,
Church Revitalization Center, The Southern Baptist Theological
Seminary

What kind of preachers do our churches need now?

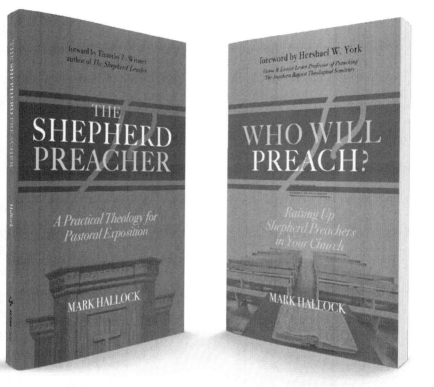

"Mark Hallock is not only passionate about seeing more shepherd preachers fill our pulpits, he is one who seeks to live it out in his own life and ministry."

Alexander Strauch, Author of *Biblical Eldership* and *Leading with Love*

ACOMA PRESS

Acoma Press exists to make Jesus non-ignorable by equipping and encouraging churches through gospel-centered resources.

Toward this end, each purchase of an Acoma Press resource serves to catalyze disciple-making and to equip leaders in God's Church. In fact, a portion of your purchase goes directly to funding planting and replanting efforts in North America and beyond. To see more of our current resources, visit us at *acomapress.org*.

Thank you.

Made in the USA
Lexington, KY
23 February 2019